**Renato De Fusco**

**Le Corbusier, Designer Furniture, 1929**

**BARRON'S**
Woodbury, New York

© 1977 Barron's Educational Series, Inc.
113 Crossways Park Drive
Woodbury, New York 11797

*Library of Congress Catalog Card No. 77-81368*

International Standard Book No. 0-8120-5148-3

Graphics: Luciano M. Boschini
Photography: Filippo Alison, Naples; Archivio fotografico
             Cassina, Meda; Antonia D'Auria, Naples;
             Fondation Le Corbusiet, Paris;
             Charlotte Perriand photographic archives, Paris
Iconographic research: Filippo Alison
In charge of design: Antonino della Gatta    Ufficio tecnico Cassina
General editor: A. Myriam Tosoni
Collection "documenti di Casabella" edited by Alessandro Mendini
Series "I Maestri" edited by Filippo Alison

Copyright © 1976
Gruppo Editoriale Electa S.p.A.
Milan, via Goldoni 1

Printed in Italy by Grafiche Milani, Segrate

# Contents

Foreword by Filippo Alison                                                    4

Le Corbusier, Designer, Furniture; 1929                                       6
   Biographical Notes                                          7
   Le Corbusier's Theory of Decorative Art                      10
   From Theory to Practice                                      17
   Furniture as "Signs"                                         28
   The Furniture Exhibited in 1929                              30
   The Historical Background of Le Corbusier's Furniture        43
   Le Corbusier's Furniture Today                               48

Models and Production                                                         56
   Siège à dossier basculant                                    58
   Fauteuil grand confort, Petit modèle                         62
   Fauteuil grand confort, Grand modèle                         62
   Chaise-longue à réglage continu                              68
   Canapé                                                       78
   Table en tube d'avion, section ovoide                        82
   Table dalle de marbre posée sur piètement acier et fonte laquée   86
   Siège tournant (Fauteuil)                                    90
   Siège tournant (Tabouret)                                    90
   Meubles acier (Casiers modulés), 1928                        94
   Casiers modulés (Meubles acier), 1935                        97

Le Corbusier and Us: An article published in *L'architetto*,
on the occasion of Le Corbusier's death                                       100

In its own sphere of existence, the impact of the creative energy of Le Corbusier against the restrictive reality of modern organizations of productive activity raises a number of questions that appear not to have been entirely resolved.

When we attempt to re-examine these questions, however, we seem to come against a certain timid reticence. Although a slavish adherence to the "cause and effect" line of reasoning often leads to contradictory conclusions, one cannot help wondering, for example, if it is true that the well-known attitude of Le Corbusier toward environmental problems—from the vast concepts of town planning and landscaping to the small-scale objects of domestic use—is utopian or anachronistic, and if so to what extent, since his plans, even those acknowledged to be the most appropriate and important for modern architecture, remained on paper and in all likelihood will never be executed.

Yet Le Corbusier had considerable expectations from the new industrial processes; he wrote in his Eastern Journey: "We defend straightforward modern technology and declare how much the arts owe to it in expressive plasticity. . . ." It must be believed that the confident optimism with which he greeted the limitless flexibility of the new metal sections unfolded to him the possibility of creating a physical environment that would make the home come closer to fulfilling the human needs of the masses. This explains why the idea of architecture came to signify for Le Corbusier what he developed out of his early meditations, where the homes of peasants and the poor engaged his attention. The bare simplicity of the dwellings at Sur or of the mosques in Istanbul, and peasant and popular art in general, appeared to him as the perfect example of the transfer of human feelings and needs into physical reality.

We certainly do not mean to view Le Corbusier's youthful enthusiasm for popular art in the light of a populist conception of the history of architecture. Le Corbusier was not much older than twenty when he told his friends at the Ateliers d'Art at La Chaux-de-Fonds of his inclination for the broad powerful forms found in the great popular tradition and peasant art: this was at the time of the definitive edition of that archetype of all modern ethnology, Frazer's Golden Bough (1911–15), when European pictorial art was coming under the influence of the uninhibited forms of Afro-Asian culture. It was Le Corbusier himself who showed us the way out of this difficulty, summing up the whole sequence of social problems of the past one hundred and fifty years and going beyond the apparent myth of Rousseau's "innocent savage"—in this case represented by the peasant in his moments of creative activity—in words that are still completely valid for us today: "All this [the custom of peasants preparing and building their own homes] means that the city must not in any way imitate the country; this would be like curing the patient by giving him the malady. The city must go forward and reinvent itself on its own. There is no other way."

The present study, like those in this same series on Mackintosh, Rietveld, Gaudí and Wright, which it accompanies, starts from the assumption that a considerable part of modern social production, together with the "so very ugly progress"—in the words of Jeanneret—which goes with it, represents a phase of historical antithesis, in which modern design, including academic design, represents the negation of the cultural source from which it was created, and which it in fact rejects. The rediscovery of history by means of a reassessment of the works and objects created by the "masters" is then seen to be extremely relevant. By this means it becomes possible to distinguish in the creative activity of these innovators the considerations, the connections, the impacts and obstacles in their relationship with social and economic reality and to set in motion a wide range of activities arising out of the analysis of different methods of planning and construction.

In this study, interest is concentrated more closely on the individualization of theoretical ideas than on the evaluation of the message. By re-examining in this way the relationship between the significance of the objects and reality, it seeks to counterbalance the movement toward the ephemeral fashions inherent in the vicious circle of consumerism—which nurtures "forms of a sick imagination . . . the whims of a blockhead, a third-rate designer, who draws up his plans for the sole purpose of differentiating them from those designed the day before."

Here—possibly for the first time in a study of articles of furniture—Renato De Fusco adopts a method that is highly suited to a study of Le Corbusier, for whom even color was an end, not a means, a creative symbol of wide significance, and never merely descriptive. "The obsession with symbols becomes for me a type of linguistic expression, circumscribed to the value of a few words. . . . To go farther, I have acquired an idea of color as something stratified in perceptions of yellow, red or blue, violet or green, rather than signifying the detail of these combinations." Le Corbusier was writing of the ideas suggested to him by his visit to the Parthenon in his **Eastern Journey** previously mentioned.

The author proceeds to an examination and redefinition of some of the most significant design objects produced by Le Corbusier. He shows the important similarities and differences between pieces of furniture and the articles composed of standard units, and discusses the place they occupy today and in the past. This succinct yet comprehensive analysis is valuable for its many ideas relating to recent problems of design and especially for its original conclusions on points of controversy. For these reasons this study provides an invaluable contribution to the process of rediscovering for history the inherent values in the "pieces" produced by the "masters" and solving the conflict between the controversial criticism and the vitality of the design.

Filippo Alison   5

## Le Corbusier, Designer
## Furniture, 1929

Le Corbusier at La Chaux-de-Fonds, 1904

The interest in *design* (in the sense of the word which will be defined later) shown by the most versatile of contemporary architects was limited compared with his interest in the sectors of architecture and town planning, or even in theoretical writings. However, the "decorative arts"—to use the outmoded expression intentionally—not only came within the general framework of his activity, but in fact initiated it. Yet this field of activity has so far not been sufficiently examined so as to define, adequately at least, if not exhaustively, the figure of Le Corbusier as a designer.

To study Le Corbusier's contribution to design by concentrating only on the best-known examples of his work in this field—the group of furniture exhibited at the 1929 Salon d'Automne or the design for the "auto maximum" which was the forerunner for many Citroën models, or even other less well-documented designs—would be to encounter only the classical "tip of the iceberg." It is highly probable that by the side of these very well-known examples there lay a wealth of ideas, projects and sketches, although these were subordinate to his large-scale projects of architecture and town planning, and confirmation of this conjecture will be provided by the research now being undertaken. In the second place, these few examples were preceded by a book, *L'Art Décoratif d'Aujourd'hui*, which gives us ample information, at least for the time when it was written, concerning Le Corbusier's theory of design and the start of his career in this sector, which in fact represented the start of his whole artistic career.

Le Corbusier with Amédée Ozenfant and Pierre Jeanneret, 1923–24

*Le Corbusier with Amédée Ozenfant, 1923–24*

## Biographical notes

We may look first at some biographical notes to be found in the chapter entitled "Confession," forming a sort of appendix to the book just referred to. They show how, almost alone and unaided, Le Corbusier traversed the evolution of the entire Modern Movement, the movement which extends from applied arts to town planning.

"Twenty-five years have passed," he wrote, "since I decided in my young mind to occupy myself with art. If today [this was in 1925, and five years later he was to say that the architectural revolution was completed and his main concern had become the revolution in town planning] I have arrived at architecture, it is after having passed through the phases of art where a greater liberty seems to reign, where contact with nature is direct and the emotions more immediate. Around 1900, when I was part of the heroic-conquistador movement, I realized a priori that only the decorative arts would engage me seriously; the 'liberal arts' seemed too inclined to absolutism. Everyone was talking about a renewal of the social system, and painting was concerned only in filtering rays of sunlight through the leafy branches of indolent landscapes. . . ."[1]

However, Le Corbusier began his career as a naturalist painter, but immediately transferred to the sphere of decorative art. In his early years at least this was always derived from nature as an organic-functional synthesis, and an echo of Ruskin may be clearly heard in many of his early experiences: "There were about twenty of us who chose our vocation: sculpture in stone or wood, ceramics, mosaics, work in glass, brass-work, engraving, carving, work in iron and gold, fresco

*Designs for carvings (1901), studies of fir trees (1902) and shells (1903)*

painting, etc. What a cohort! Boundless joy in living, total faith . . . 'Here,' said the Master, 'we will construct a monument dedicated to nature. To it we will consecrate the aim of our lives. We shall leave the towns and go to live among the lofty woods, beneath the edifice which we shall gradually fill with our works. . . .' Many art studios were established in those years. We decorated chapels, concert halls, created furniture and jewels, and built grave monuments for cemeteries. Most of us had left our families and rented barns in the city outskirts to which we went at night in order to be closer to nature. . . . We had founded a school (rather like the Weimar Bauhaus ten years later)."[2]

It seems really strange that the man who was to become the main defender of the large metropolis had in the first years of his artistic career so intensely shared the desire to escape the town and immerse himself romantically in nature. Equally strange appears the later superimposing of the school of Van de Velde and Gropius onto the Ruskinian *Guild* model.

After this youthful community of craftsmen broke up, Le Corbusier proceeded to complete his education on his own, first through the discovery of museums and then by travel.

Speaking of museums, he said that he looked at the works of Cimabue, Brueghel, Raphael, Tintoretto, etc., but his interest had been attracted mainly by the tapestries, the dishes, the gods made of bronze, wood or stone, the doorways of cathedrals, shells, birds, the huge skeletons of prehistoric and present-day animals, and he described these experiences as his "first introduction to the mechanical interrelationship of objects."[3]

His travels ranged over the countries of middle Europe, the East and the Mediterranean. Referring to the first, he records his meeting with Perret, who advised him to engage in mathematics and to follow the precept that "it is necessary to construct with perfection; generally decoration masks a lack of construction."[4] But it was during a visit to Germany, where Le Corbusier had been given the task of researching the decorative arts, that for the first time he came into contact with the world of industry. He came to understand the modern organization of labor and the anachronism presented by the figure of the artist-decorator in such a context. In reference to this figure, he remarked, "Is it possible for decorators, by means of sketches made on paper, and following where their imagination leads them, to modify the fatal, almost automatic, rigor of the modern industrial process? Can the industrial product be correct, when it is thrown into confusion by interference from outside? Has the decorator—whom I admired at that

Notes
[1] Le Corbusier, *L'Art D'ecoratif d'Aujourd'hui* (It. trans. *Arte decorativa e design*, Laterza, Bari, 1973, pp. 199–200)
[2] Ibid., pp. 200–201
[3] Ibid., p. 211
[4] Ibid.
[5] Ibid., p. 213
[6] Ibid., p. 214
[7] Ibid., p. 219

*Watch made of gold, silver and copper engraved by Charles-Edouard Jeanneret at the age of 15*

time—the right to this enormous claim?"[5] These doubts led Le Corbusier to the conclusion that "the schools of decorative arts must be closed down."[6] And rejecting the developments which had occurred in the great European capitals—the results of the art nouveau movement—he started on a journey to discover the sources of art in the ancient world. After leaving Prague, he proceeded to Constantinople, Greece, South Italy and Rome.

"I have seen," he wrote in the same chapter, "Confession," of his *L'Art Décoratif d'Aujourd'hui*, "the great eternal monuments, the glory of the human spirit. I trusted especially in the invincible attraction of the Mediterranean. It was high time, after ten years . . . of decorative art and German architecture! . . . Thus I discovered architecture. Architecture is the magnificent pattern of forms as the light falls on them. Architecture is a coherent system of the mind. Architecture has nothing in common with decoration. Architecture is in the severe and splendid monuments bequeathed to us by time, just as it is in the smallest Alpine hut, in a boundary wall, or in any sublime or modest object containing enough geometry in itself to enable a mathematical relationship to be incorporated within it."[7] From the foregoing it can be said that, at least in what he writes about his own experience, Le Corbusier brought decorative art (which may provisionally be defined as design) to the level of architecture, and in this he anticipated the systematic procedure he was to follow as well as the similar leveling he was to make later between architecture and town planning. However, besides the evolution connected with his personal experiences, many more detailed and complex developments were to become part of his theory of design.

9

L'ACROPOLE A ATHENES

## Le Corbusier's theory of decorative art

In order to understand Le Corbusier's thought on the subject of design, at least so far as it was expressed at the time of the book previously mentioned, it is necessary in the first place to give thought to a question of semantics; that is, the precise meaning of the word *design*. It is known that this English word denotes "planning" in various fields, extending from town planning to the most diverse objects of daily use. With the passage of time this term, employed without other attributes, has more and more come to indicate the planning and production of objects, excluding architecture, or a certain type of highly industrialized architecture, consisting of the assembly of prefabricated units, etc., to which the term *design* is more applicable; so that it is these forms, and perhaps these alone, which may legitimately be described by the term *design* for the architecture which they generate, while all other types of architecture belong to a more personal and traditional classification. In the sphere of the planning and production of objects of domestic use, from furniture to lampshades, from carpets to fabrics, the term *design* has replaced the old expression *decorative art*. And it is precisely on this question of terminology that Le Corbusier's thought was focused and his theory of design came into being (although the actual word *design* does not appear in the book in question).

Speaking of decorative art, he wrote, "It should be noted that in thirty years no one has succeeded in coining an appropriate term. Could this be because this activity is so lacking in exactitude, or sense, that it is impossible to find a definition for it? The Germans have found the term *Kunstgewerbe* (industrial art), which is even more am-

10

biguous! Not to mention the pejorative term *applied art*.[8] It seemed that the very inappropriateness of this term denoted the contradictions inherent in this whole sphere of activity. Nor can it be said, to anticipate a conclusion I shall arrive at later, that the incorrect definition of decorative art was made much clearer when the term *design* was used in its place, since the latter term covered so broad a field of application that it could not be used to signify any individual one exhaustively. This was true especially of the range of objects of domestic use, a field much richer in connotations and implications than, for example, surgical instruments or articles for orthopedic use—examples which Le Corbusier himself took as a point of reference in his search for objective certainties.

After his consideration of terminology, Le Corbusier continued his attempt at theoretical clarification, in the same book, starting from the basic assumption that "modern decorative art does not comprise any kind of decoration";[9] he wondered if this idea might represent a paradox, but came to the conclusion that "the paradox is not in the fact, it is in the word. Why should we call the objects we are now considering *decorative art*? This is the paradox: why apply the term decorative art to chairs, bottles, baskets, shoes, all of which are useful objects and items of equipment?"[10]

Of course, this is more than a rhetorical question, and while the term *items of equipment* has highly polemical overtones, this does not succeed in eclipsing the products of either decorative or applied art, mainly because of the presence of the word *art* in these old-fashioned expressions and concepts. It is at this point that Le Corbusier's ideas    11 differed from the line of thought and inquiry which is conventionally grouped under the classification "from Morris to Gropius," where the question of art, as an aesthetic matter, appears frequently so to speak in parenthesis, or is entirely set aside. In contrast, Le Corbusier tackled the problem of design from the standpoint of aesthetic argument, even though he followed the line of French rationalism, that of Viollet-le-Duc in particular.

I have defined the basic principle on which his theory is based, the assumption that modern decorative art does not comprise any kind of decoration; the origin of this principle is to be found in the writings of Loos, to which Le Corbusier adds: "People say, however, that decoration is necessary. This is not so. Only art is necessary—the disinterested passion which uplifts us."[11] As can be seen, Le Corbusier distinguished art—a phenomenon and value neglected or disregarded by others, as we have just seen—from decorative art, and made a further differentiation between the decorative art of the past and that of his own time. The latter was included because of the new processes of production only if no kind of decoration was added. He continued, "In order to understand this clearly, it is necessary to separate the sensations, which are disinterested, from the needs which aim at their utilitarian gratification."[12] Elsewhere, to overcome the risk of the artistic product—the product of the "disinterested sensations"—becoming inexpressible, he remarked: "The awakening of noble sensations is determined by proportion, which is a mathematical reality experienced through the senses and supplied principally by architecture [while admitting that the latter begins where calculation ends], painting and sculpture, works of no immediate use, disinterested and exceptional; works whose physical reality becomes imbued with passion, the passion of man—the multiform drama which makes us pause, stirs and agitates us, and arouses our emotions."[13]

Then passing from art to the objects which satisfy our daily needs, Le Corbusier went on: "The equipment needed for this purpose must be perfected by industry. In this way the magnificent program of decorative art is formed. With the passage of time industry produces perfect functional and utilitarian objects, whose authentic splendor—the pleasure of the mind—emanates from the elegance of their conception, the simplicity of their execution, and their effectiveness in use. . . . And we shall see that this decorative art without decoration is not the work of artists, but of anonymous industry, which proceeds lightly and airily along the path of the economy."[14]

So that against the trend of the mass of decorators who were still operating with outmoded concepts, against the romantic school of Ruskin, the adherents of art nouveau, the Masters of the twentieth century and *Arts Déco*—(in other words, the very style practiced at the 1925 *Exposition Internationale*)—Le Corbusier saw that the pattern for modern design was to be found in industrial methods of production, with their "logic" and technology. And to illustrate this idea, he enriched the pages of his *L'Art Décoratif d'Aujourd'hui* with a whole series of industrial objects: turbines, cars, medical and hospital equip-

creative model, there is thus only a difference of degree between the two.[15] But Le Corbusier was not Gropius, and in the early 1920s he seemed less anxious to contribute to the setting up of teams of designers than to find arguments which could be adapted to a mass culture. Meanwhile he described the machine, or rather the whole industrial process, as the model of a self-sufficient productive organism, which rather like a virgin birth creates objects whose nature determines the style of our period.

Of course, he did not deny that the machine must be guided by man, and in fact stated that in the machine man had at last found something to work in his place, so allowing him more time for work which is truly creative. On the other hand, he stated explicitly that the machine possesses its own specific quality and autonomy, revealing the emptiness of the conventional decorative formulas employed by the romantic artists as well as unmasking the deception whereby decoration was used to conceal a weakness of execution. However paradoxical it might appear, the idea of an industrial virgin birth is not entirely without foundation, nor is it ineffectual in reinforcing his argument. For is there such a thing as industrial production which proceeds of its own volition? Stated negatively, it is the desire of the labor force to reproduce the models of the past by the use of the new techniques, a process from which innovators and planners are excluded. Stated positively, it is the desire of responsible industrialists to produce new types of objects, whose form is dictated purely by function, and here again, in the period we are considering, the innovators and planners were not yet prepared for this task.

Le Corbusier's reference to the autonomy of industry and specifically to that part of production which comes into being without the aid of the artist-decorator recalls those moments in political history when society, with all its limits, contradictions, class conflicts, etc., seems to be self-perpetuating, making do without a political class, which often shows itself inadequate to meet the demands made upon it. And there can be no doubt that in many periods of its history, within its restricted and narrow compass, the world of industry has shown greater imagination and creativity than the art experts, and greater efficiency than the experts in political administration. What in fact is meant by the autonomy of the machine is the autonomy and "creativity" of the producer. And—although this fact does not appear in history manuals—it is the producer who in practice bears the aesthetic and social responsibility, for better or worse, for the birth and development of design. This was the thought behind Le Cor-

*Industrially produced objects illustrated in the book* L'Art Décoratif d'Aujourd'hui. *On the left, wardrobe-trunk "Innovation"; above, steel chest Ormo*

ment, airplanes, interior décor for American banks, metal furniture, footwear, and the famous Hermès leatherware.

Concerning the relationship between crafts and industry, Benevolo has made the apt comment that Gropius did not choose between one term and the other, but believed that they expressed a kind of battle between two opposed abstractions. Indeed, since it cannot be said that crafts exist purely as abstract ideas, the ideas of the craftsman having to be expressed by means of a technical process, while industry is not purely mechanical, its products having to be based on a

13

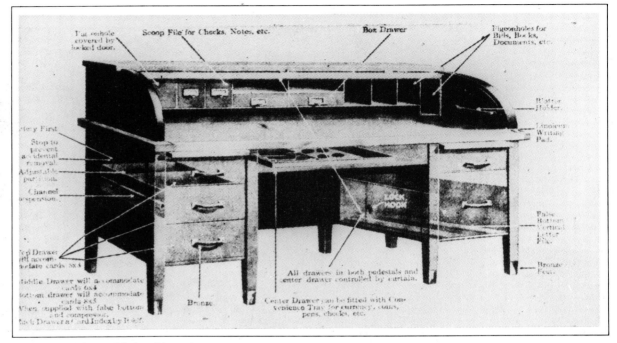

busier's *Appel aux Industriels*, with its echo of the ideas of Saint Simon. As for the social and political developments connected with this position, Le Corbusier did not seem much concerned over them, here, too, trusting in a sort of self-regulation, which was expressed, for example, in the aphorism: "Now the gilt is disappearing, and before very long the hovel too will disappear."[16]

In contrast to the view held by the German expressionists and rationalists, that industry was a collective force for good, containing the potential, partly spiritual, of achieving a more equable distribution of the wealth of nature, the *machinisme* of Le Corbusier appears less idealistic and oversimplified. He did not have behind him the support of social historians like Max Weber, or people like Rathenau who believed in progressive enterprise, the group concept of the Werkbund, and least of all the German desire for a revival of past glories. But more than his German colleagues Le Corbusier possessed the strength of great aesthetic ideals, in the broader but necessarily less precise meaning of the term, associated with a keen feeling for the

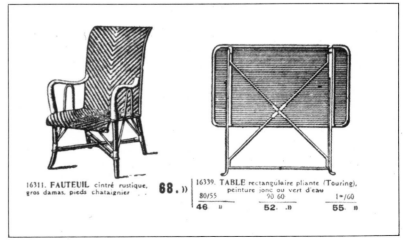

16311. FAUTEUIL cintré rustique, gros damas, pieds chataignier . . . **68.** »

16339. TABLE rectangulaire pliante (Touring), peinture jonc ou vert d'eau

| 80/55 | 90 60 | 1=/60 |
|-------|-------|-------|
| **46** » | **52.** » | **55.** » |

*Notes*
[8]*Le Corbusier, Op. cit.*, p. 86
[9]Ibid., p. 85
[10]Ibid.
[11]Ibid., p. 86
[12]Ibid.
[13]Ibid., p. 87
[14]Ibid., pp. 83–92
[15]Cf. L. Benevolo, *Storia dell'architettura moderna*, Laterza, Bari, 1973, p. 450
[16]*Le Corbusier, Op. cit.*, p. 41
[17]Ibid., p. 113

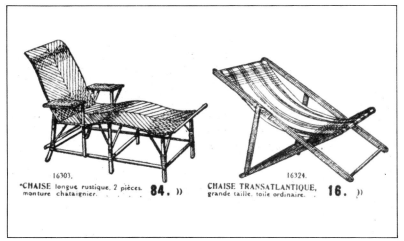

"CHAISE longue rustique, 2 pièces. **84.** »
monture chataignier.     16303.

CHAISE TRANSATLANTIQUE, **16.** »
grande taille, toile ordinaire.     16324.

historical situation of his time, and he directed these qualities to the pursuance of a new trend and to persuading others to accept it. And it may perhaps be said that from this starting point, with its relative limitations, and aiming towards these goals, in the long run the ideas of Le Corbusier will be found more appropriate and effective at a social level also, as is shown by the fact that in many respects they anticipate the mass culture of today.

After this brief mention of social factors, let us return specifically to Le Corbusier's theory of decorative art, and ask ourselves a question intended to reconcile and explain the duality between the creative worker and the industrial organization: does there not perhaps exist a "structure," having something in common with the work of the former and the productivity of the latter? Le Corbusier spoke of a "hidden sentiment": "The machine is calculation; calculation is the human creative system contained in our being, which explains and proves precisely to our understanding the universe which we apprehend intuitively, and nature which we see in the tangible 15

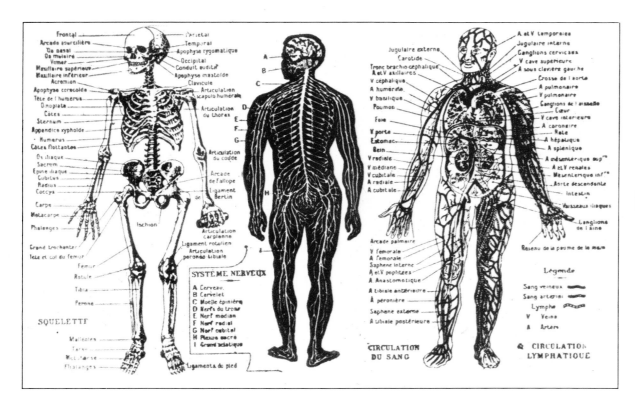

*Studies of the human body from* L'Art Décoratif d'Aujourd'hui.

manifestations of an ordered life. The graphic expression of this calculation is geometry, our very own method, precious to us, the only means we have of measuring facts and objects. The machine comes entirely out of geometry. Geometry, our great invention, the invention which exalts us."[17]

Calculation and geometry, taken as the essentially human medium for man to use in measuring himself against nature and deception, this hidden value containing a certain *Einfühlung,* as well as an aesthetic idea, represents a real principle of structure, which serves also, in a most tangible way, to bring the problem of design to the level of architecture. And here too Le Corbusier departs from his German colleagues, who in their most significant works and writings brought architecture to the level of design, whereas Le Corbusier did just the opposite.

## From theory to practice

Le Corbusier based his designs on three principal ideas: *(a)* the standard unit; *(b)* furniture and tools viewed as artificial limbs; *(c)* the new technology.

"Leaving behind the unquiet reign of fantasy and the incongruous, we can regain possession of a comforting set of norms. . . . To seek for the human level, the human function, means to define human needs. These needs are few in number, identical in all men, since from time immemorial man has been made from the same stamp. . . . *These needs are standard*, that is, they are the same for everybody; we all need to complete our natural capacities by reinforcing elements."[18]

The notion of a standard is common to all the theory of Le Corbusier, and those who know his architecture will have encountered it many times; in the field of design, however, it gives rise to a new suggestion, which is that objects of design should be thought of as artificial limbs. But before going on to these topics, let us pause briefly to consider the other basic principle that all men are equal and have the same needs.

It can be said that it was this fundamental assumption of rationalism, and the rationalism of Le Corbusier in particular, that drew the attacks of academic criticism and even more so by the post-rationalist movements, accusing Le Corbusier of abstraction, of little historical awareness, since in history it is the individual and the exception which hold the dominating role, and of taking no account of psychological motivations, etc. Yet, while the limitations of the assumption that men are equal are so obvious that they were known even to those who upheld it—so that it is hypocritical to pretend shock—could there not have been in this principle another aspect applicable to the reform of architecture and applied arts, namely the concept of the "standard" as a means of concentrating all the efforts of the planners on a few prototypes which could be produced by industrial processes and extended over the whole social sphere? If it be true that behind every process (in our case the history of the Modern Movement) there is a system (in our case the code of practice of Le Corbusier), based on a few basic assumptions, then these assumptions could not be other than those just indicated. This is because these are the only ones which are capable of reconciling the most basic and widely shared human necessities with those of modern industrial technology and economy, and to reconcile them without disregarding questions of taste and style. As Le Corbusier expressed it: "There is a new spirit, a spirit of construction and synthesis directed by a clear conception."[19] Needless to say, no one still nurtures this optimistic faith, a faith which triumphs in the time to which it belongs, because we have seen the other side of this "spirit" and "clear conception." But while it is true that we show less ingenuousness, we are at the same time less enthusiastic; and the loss of enthusiasm is a great drawback, leading possibly to the loss of all creativity.

To turn to point *(b)* of our summary, that is that furniture and tools should be thought of as artificial limbs, Le Corbusier thought that objects of this nature must follow the line laid down by tailors, by car body builders, cinema set designers and manufacturers of household articles. Our minds are different, but our bodies and muscle structure are similar and fulfill the same functions. For this reason objects of decorative art must respond to typical needs and typical functions, and therefore be typical objects. Le Corbusier declared that the closer such objects come to our bodies in contact and function the more they may be likened to artificial limbs; this realization led him to the conclusion that decorative art represents a kind of orthopedics. Several considerations emerge from this concept.

It clearly derives from the precepts of the naturalist Lamarck, especially his view that form must follow function, and confers a scientific basis to Le Corbusier's argument. It had been of interest to both the precursors and the practitioners of the Modern Movement, while at the same time it held an attraction for the general public who were fascinated by the myth of the natural sciences. So that the fact that his theory fitted in with the criteria of science represented a common bond between the innovators of design—or at least the *avant-garde* of research—and the general public, and Le Corbusier made the most of this in his propaganda campaign.

In the second place, the *esprit machiniste* contained in this idea has within it a criticism of all that is ephemeral and sham in "decoration," an aversion which Le Corbusier explicitly stated having received from Loos. In the third place, as already mentioned, there was an interest and liking for certain categories of objects which came to be taken more or less as models. In particular one thinks of orthopedic furniture, reclining seats, surgical instruments, in other words, products whose creation was decided purely by function and represented the fruits of "patient research" (another well-known theme beloved of Le Corbusier). No decorator, no "artist" has intervened in their slow process of development and modification, yet no one can dispute the fact that they possess a validity of their own, even on the aesthetic plane. It is true that this aesthetic validity is that of the closest adherence of form to function, but once the rationalists took these objects out of context, following the example of the innovators in the arts (Dadaism, surrealism and even purism itself), that is, when they transferred them from the realm of technical objects to the domestic sphere, they came to acquire a new aesthetic connotation. The old refrain still repeated by the bourgeoisie—this room all in white, with its metal furniture, is like a hospital ward—must have been well known even to the first rationalists and it is quite probable that this trivial comment may actually have inspired them. In fact, what is a hospital ward if not a perfect "machine," not only a machine to live in, but also to recover in? One of Le Corbusier's many aphorisms, used in another context, may legitimately be applied to the matter we are considering: "Since we have no wish to die, the simple desire to live will make us return to health and from there, on to beauty."[20]

The forms which may be associated with the concept of objects as prolongations of our limbs are, moreover, reinforced by the new technology (point *c* of our summary). Le Corbusier questioned the exclusive use of wood in furniture, and wished to put in its place steel, aluminum, cement, and synthetic fibers. In his view, furniture apprentices should leave the Faubourg Saint-Antoine and go instead to Levallois, or Issy-les-Moulineaux, where planes and cars are manufactured. Completely new techniques were employed in their manufacture which made the articles more hardwearing and enabled them to be arranged in a new way. It was here, declared Le Corbusier, that metal furniture was born; it existed already in offices, but was now brought into use in the home, in cupboards, seats, tables, etc. The "parlor" of yesteryear had faded away; a new furniture age was born.

As we see, the same slogans which had been applied to architecture and town planning were found in exact replica in the field of design, especially as related to objects of domestic use. But here too Le Corbusier did not confine himself to suggesting new forms for individual articles (although he did this later, as we shall see in detail), but indicated a whole new conception of furnishing the home: the arrangement took over from the room, or, more precisely, preordained the room, within which the furniture was to play a special role.

At the meeting place between architecture and design stands the *équipement* of the home, a new term taking the place of the word *mobilier.* The basis of the new equipment was the standard unit *(casier standard)*—cupboards composed of sections of equal size which were fit-

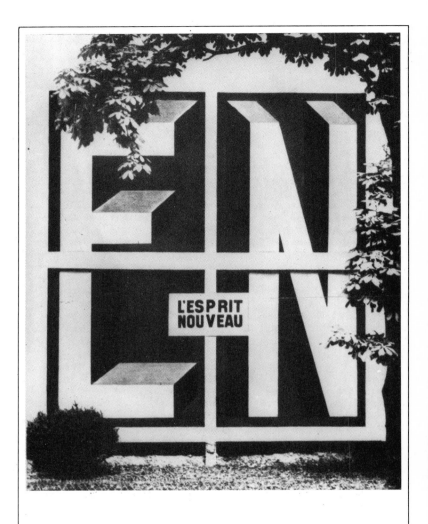

*Exterior of the Esprit Nouveau pavilion, 1925*

*Interior of the Esprit Nouveau pavilion, 1925*

ted together. These could be built into the wall, stand against it or act as a partition between one room and another. The idea for them was taken from office furniture, but in their domestic version they were used essentially as containers for any type of object, as required for the type of room in which they were placed. They took the place of a group of pieces of furniture, *les innombrables meubles affublés aux formes et aux noms variés*, and by making available the maximum amount of space inside them, left the maximum bare space in the room. Beds, tables, and the various types of chairs especially, remained masters of the field; the room was completely bare of any other types of container, so that these pieces could act as sculpture in space, and since they are the pieces of furniture which come into the most direct contact with the human body, their arrangement could be modified to determine various situations in the life of the home.

In effect, the interior of the home was classified in two categories of objects: furniture objects—different from the traditional ones in form, function, arrangement and the technique by which they were produced—and the units called by Le Corbusier *casiers standard*. And this duality between furniture and standard units is found present in the construction and appearance of all the architecture of Le Corbusier.

As previously stated,[21] the latter may be divided into two family groups: one, representing most of the buildings, where the dominant feature is a sense of geometric precision, the standard, pure stereometry and order—the group belonging, one might say, to the spirit of Descartes—and the other group comprising the so-called "free forms" (the molding of the stilts, the equipment for roof gardens, certain freer subdivisions of the inner area of rooms—for example, circular staircases and the archways linking one pillar to the next, etc.). On another occasion I have pointed out that the former group arose directly out of geometrical studies, out of calculation and the functions related to the theory of rationalism, while the latter (which was sometimes the model for whole buildings, the Ronchamp Chapel, for example, although some people have mistaken this for an expressionist work or a rejection of the whole of Le Corbusier's style so far) was directly linked to the contemporary artistic developments in the fields of painting and sculpture, in the purist period, which later turned to brutalism—and possibly the influence of Picasso played some part too.

Having made this distinction, it becomes easy to place the *casiers standard* in the first family, where they are seen to be closer to archi-   19

*From left to right:*
*Drawing by Amédée Ozenfant, 1926*
*Le Corbusier, Still Life with Numerous Objects, 1923*
*Le Corbusier, Vertical Guitar, 1920*
*Le Corbusier, Still Life, 1925*

Notes
[18]*Le Corbusier, Op. cit.* p. 71–73
[19]Ibid., p. 222
[20]Ibid., p. 220
[21]Cf. R. De Fusco, *Storia dell'architettura contemporanea*, Laterza, Bari, 1974

tecture than are separate pieces of furniture—upright chairs, armchairs or tables—which are more closely allied to the plastic forms of sculpture and painting. But let us examine more closely the products of these two categories.

The *casiers standard*, the cupboard standard units, made their first appearance, if I am not mistaken, at the *Esprit Nouveau* pavilion in the 1925 Paris Exhibition; but they were still at an early stage of development and were in the form of standard parallelepipeds supported by simple legs of metal tubing, and designed as room partitions. In the 1929 Salon d'Automne—where they were exhibited together with nearly all the furniture made the year previously in collaboration with Charlotte Perriand and the faithful Pierre Jeanneret (this is the furniture which represents Le Corbusier's greatest contribution to this field)—the *casiers standard* were developed in a mainly quantitative di-

20

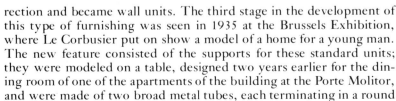

rection and became wall units. The third stage in the development of this type of furnishing was seen in 1935 at the Brussels Exhibition, where Le Corbusier put on show a model of a home for a young man. The new feature consisted of the supports for these standard units; they were modeled on a table, designed two years earlier for the dining room of one of the apartments of the building at the Porte Molitor, and were made of two broad metal tubes, each terminating in a round base large enough to contain the movements of the table when it was pushed sideways. We see therefore that Le Corbusier adopted the same principle of stilts as he used in his architecture in order to support the 1935 standard units and partitions. In this third version, then, this type of furniture shared the characteristics of each of the two family groupings previously described: the stereometric body may be related to the "Cartesian" aspect of the buildings, while the

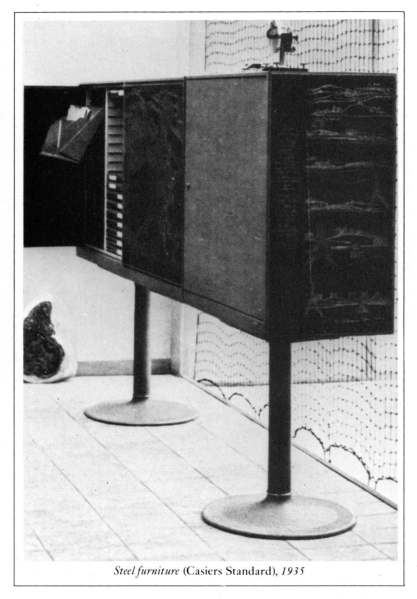

*Steel furniture* (Casiers Standard), *1935*

supports—so anomalous and "brutalist," as were numerous examples of stilts—belong to the free forms of purist artistic origin.

These *casiers standard*, which became so highly successful as all-purpose containers that they have become an essential part of every present-day interior (in fact there is no building enterprise today which fails to provide fixtures of this type in its rooms), have unfortunately not been successful in the sense anticipated by Le Corbusier, and it must be asked why this should have been the case. What, for example, has become now of the type of metal furniture which is so perfect in its execution that it permitted of very few personal changes on the part of those who were to use it, once it was placed in a setting such as a wall or room divider? Why is it that this type of furniture, which was derived from offices, should have successfully retained its position in its original setting but made little impact on the furnishings of the home?

These questions point to the rigidity of the concept of functionalism and the limitations this imposes. In a home there is a need for the occupants to be able to adapt the furniture to their own taste, however ill-founded or subjective their motivations might be, so that when they came upon the completely "prearranged" setting of the functionalist concept, this need was bound to be thwarted. This is true even though the functionalists always proclaimed their interest in the types of structures and objects which could be freely moved around in space, be interchangeable, etc. In other words, if wall units may be said to have originated in the ideas of functionalism, then they were received and used by the public as such, without any of the numerous connotations inherent in this type of furniture by way of materials, flexibility, uniformity, etc.; it is therefore not at all surprising that furniture resembling the *casiers standard* invented by Le Corbusier appears today in the form of wood with decorative motifs, fabrics, or even wallpaper.

To anticipate some considerations of a semeiotic* nature, the *casiers standard* are essentially a hybrid: they are clearly not an architectonic "sign" (the definition of this will be given later) nor are they to be considered conventional autonomous signs of the type represented by sculptures, or design objects such as actual pieces of furniture. They belong as much to the category of architecture, because they help to shape and subdivide in a certain way the area of the room, as to that of *design*, or furniture, because they contain objects but do not create a space which can be occupied on a human scale. Because of this ambiguity, they are always directly dependent upon an architectonic space

*Furnishings of a room, Salon d' Automne, Paris, 1929. Living room*

*Vestibule and studio of Le Corbusier's apartment in Rue Nungesser et Coli, Paris, 1938*

and therefore do not possess the autonomy which characterizes the individual article of furniture. For the features they still retain of the old cupboards, they form part of the category of furniture, while for their function of defining or subdividing living areas they belong to the category of architectonic "supports," in the same way as walls. Thus they are theoretically and morphologically more correct the closer they approach one or the other camps: either boldly declaring their function to be furniture, or else "hiding" in the walls, that is to say, when they are seen as "sub-signs" of the architectonic "sign."

The very opposite may be said of articles of furniture of traditional type, and in addition to a critical description I shall attempt a semeiological analysis, and take the opportunity to make an examination of this type, possibly the first time this has been done in relation to the field of design.

24

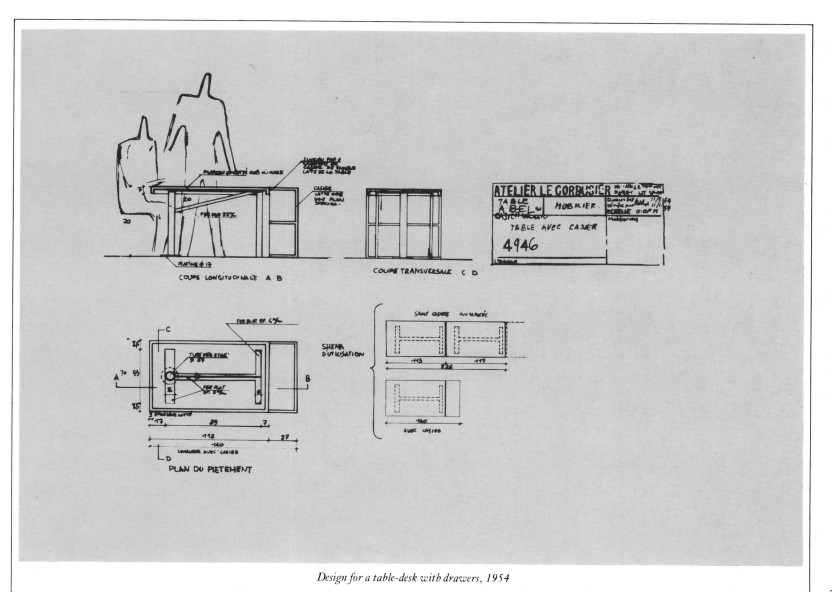

*Design for a table-desk with drawers, 1954*

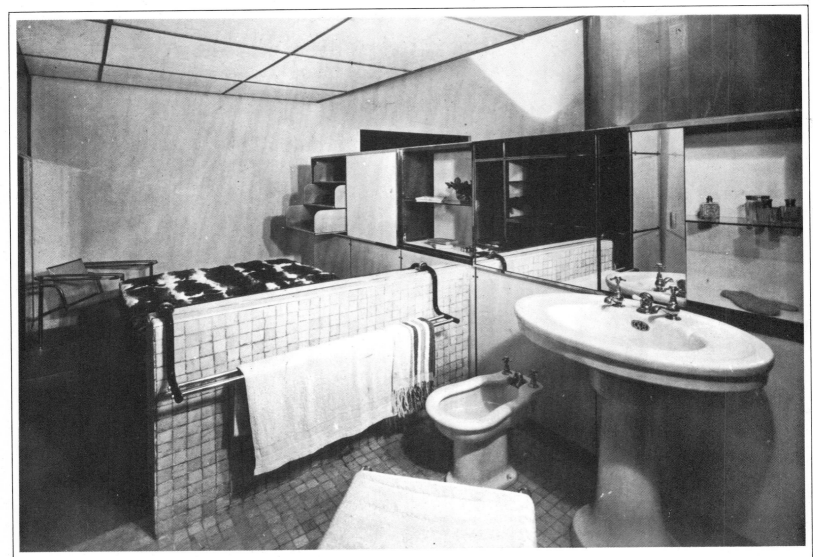

*Bathroom furnishings, Salon d'Automne, Paris, 1929*

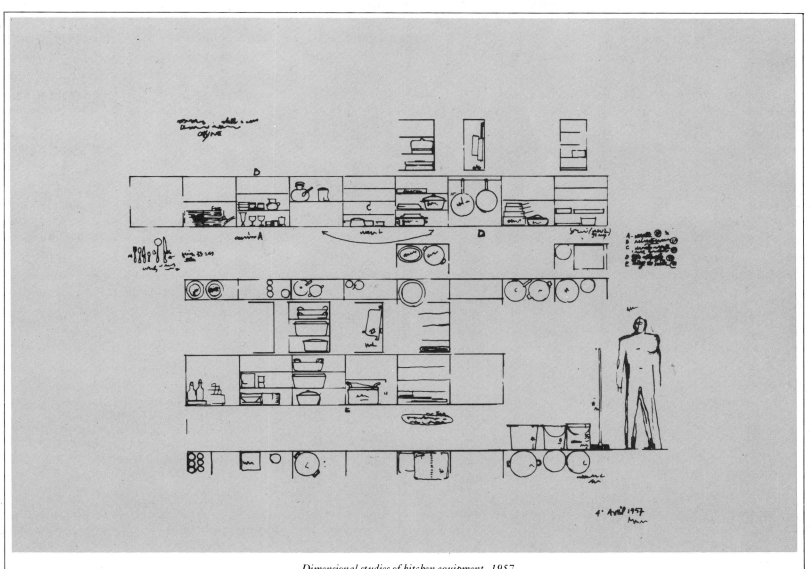

*Dimensional studies of kitchen equipment, 1957*

## Furniture as "signs"

It was Sergio Bettini who first spoke of furniture in this sense, and it was of Le Corbusier he was thinking: "It seems to me," he wrote, "that the greatest quality of these armchairs by Le Corbusier is that they are 'signs', where the two symbolic links of space and time ('geometry' and 'function,' or, to quote Pascal out of context, 'esprit de géométrie' and 'esprit de finesse') are brought together, through the 'word' of Le Corbusier, to form an impeccable equilibrium."[22]

Now it seems to me that a recourse to semeiotic analysis—while recognizing the fact that previous studies by the present author may have resulted in conditioning his view of it—can prove an indispensable aid to the exercise of criticism, just as in any other field of knowledge one must not disregard the most recent findings, even though one may not agree with them.

Starting from this point, I take up the results or suggestions of some of the best Italian semeiologists in connection with design. In particular, these authors have no hesitation in identifying architecture and design in their semeiological formulations, even though they can then proceed to analyze an object belonging to one or the other groups as if they were completely autonomous. G. K. Koenig wrote in 1964: "We must ask ourselves if even the 'Barcelona' chair by Mies, a clothes iron, a car, are architectonic signs, or in fact everything which we group under the term *industrial design*. Of course, in common usage the term *architecture* has a much more limited application and cannot be referred to these objects. . . . Besides, if we wished to separate conceptually the objects of industrial design from architecture, we would find ourselves in a further difficulty, since all the signs belonging to these two categories have a form which responds to a *utilitas*, that is, they have their own function. But since the purpose they denote is the same, for even the signs belonging to the same type of language have two homogeneous meanings . . . it must be understood that from now onwards every time the reader sees the word *architecture* he will have to understand that all the linguistic arguments applied to refer to architecture may equally be extended to cover all categories of designs—in other words, everything which can be planned, designed, and executed to be of use to man."[23] In 1968 U. Eco wrote: "Let it be clear that from now on the expression *architecture* will be used to cover the phenomena of architecture proper, of design and of town planning." And he added, "We shall leave in abeyance for the moment the question of whether the definitions we shall give can later

be applied to any planning for the modification of reality on a three-dimensional level for the purpose of allowing the fulfillment of some particular function connected with its associated life."[24]

Now, apart from Eco's precaution in postponing a decision concerning a sector in which in my opinion it is correct to place design, the lack of hesitation on the part of both writers in identifying architecture with design is the result of two convictions, one historical, the other more precisely semeiotic. The former is based on the idea held by many masters of the Modern Movement, and even more so by its interpreters, that architecture and design are subject to a single method and a single functional purpose, so that it is quite legitimate to refer to them synonymously. But for how many people today is such an assumption still valid? Is this perhaps not one of those areas where after several crises the Modern Movement has shown the greatest weakness? The second reason for the belief held by these writers lies in the concept that the significance of the architectural sign is its function. "Our semeiological position," declared Eco, "recognizes in the architectural sign the presence of a signifying factor whose signified factor is the function which it renders possible."[25] In other words, an object can be said to exist—whether of the type of architecture, design or town planning—which is produced in the first place in order to fulfill a function and in the second place in order to communicate: but to communicate what? Firstly, its denoted significance, that is, its function, and, secondly, its connoted significance, which is everything that particular shape leads us to associate with it mentally.

With the problem stated in these terms, it would seem that one might legitimately consider architecture and design in the same way, seeing them as manifestations of one language. But this is not the way I see it. For if from a rigorously structuralist viewpoint we can always set up for ourselves an abstract system in which to place one or another class of objects, without verification, on the other hand when we come to analyze in detail a real system of objects it is necessary to establish either a field of application defining the scope of the analysis—that is, here too we must make a model—or else we must recognize links and invariables in that system, so that it becomes possible to define it as a system of architectonic, urbanistic or design signs, etc. At first glance, as previously stated, design seems to come into the sphere of the types of planning for the modification of reality at a three-dimensional level for the purpose of allowing the fulfillment of a particular function connected with its associated life, of which Eco speaks, though thinking of other systems.

Dorfles in his turn agrees with the semeiotics of design being put together with that of architecture. "Many of the symbolic and semantic aspects of design," according to him, "form part of a broader question linked to the semeiological position of architectonic criticism, which can easily be extended to include design too."[26] This author is in agreement too in identifying the "significance" of a design object with its function, lending support to this generalized view with reasons of his own which merit quotation. Speaking of the industrial object's particular symbolism, he refers to that "property whereby the object is led, and in fact destined from its first conception, to 'signify its function' in a manner which is completely apparent through the significance imparted to a three-dimensional element which is able to stress that type of figuration that from time to time serves to indicate to us the characteristic function of the object. For this reason we shall finally be able to sustain the view that the concept of 'functionalism'— at one time thought to be the determining factor in an industrially produced object—may be replaced by the semantic concept: in other words, in order to be functional in the real sense of the word, an object not only will have to meet practical and utilitarian demands, be suited to the characteristics of the material employed, have regard to cost, etc.—but must also fulfill *semeiotic demands, concerned with the relation between the form of the object and its significance*."[27]

This old formula which links form to function, here enriched by semeiotic terminology, has been contested by me in relation to architectural semeiology; but in the field of design it seems to have greater validity. Indeed, in view of the single functional purpose of a design object, and the most immediate and obvious usage for which it was intended, it would seem that its function is related to its form in the same way as the "signified" and "signifying" elements defined by Saussure. [Saussure was an authority on linguistics.—TRANSLATOR] But this is not the case. To say that the form of a spoon "signifies" the function of eating liquid soup is to go no farther than the most obvious of empirical considerations. As soon as we try to penetrate the sense of that object a little more deeply, we have to do much more: we must analyze it not only according to the material parts which make it up but also following a pattern of opposed terms fixed by a structural model, or an abstract system and code of reference, with respect to which the object will begin to reveal itself as a communicative act, a message. If this were not the case, once the function of the object "spoon" had been fixed for ever—and note that we are speaking of a form whose use is almost limited to a single purpose—how could we

Notes
*Semeiotic or semeiological relating to the language of signs—TRANS.
[22]S. Bettini, in *Le Corbusier e il "Design" moderno*, in "Le Corbusier"/Cassina, 1965
[23]G. K. Koenig, *Analisi del linguaggio architettonico*, Libreria editrice fiorentina, Florence, 1964, pp. 61–62
[24]U. Eco, *La struttura assente*, Bompiani, Milan, 1968, p. 191
[25]Ibid., p. 200
[26]G. Dorfles, *Introduzione al disegno industriale*, Einaudi, Turin, 1972, pp. 49–50
[27]Ibid., pp. 47–51

explain the infinite varieties of shape presented by such an object at all levels?

But once the semeiological unity of architecture and design has been questioned, and it has been acknowledged that the notion of the "signified element" = "function" is insufficient, how should one individualize the specific semeiotic nature of the sector now under consideration? Can we apply the same dichotomies and oppositions as I have singled out in relation to other sectors which were the objects of earlier studies of mine?

I should not like to overload a short essay on the figure of Le Corbusier the designer, and specifically relating to the furniture he produced in 1929, by a theoretical treatise which is out of place here. However, before we proceed farther, the following points should be borne in mind: *(a)* design is a language with points in common with architecture, but is by no means to be identified with it; *(b) design*, in its general acceptation, designates too vast a phenomenology to be reduced to a single type of language; *(c)* the part of design which comes closest to architecture, that is, interior design and objects of domestic use, may be still too broad and heterogeneous to permit of a single type of semeiotic analysis. What is certain is that a given system of objects will lend itself to semeiological analysis if, and only if, we are able to define at least its specific "sign."

It can be seen that even from these brief considerations there emerge more questions than answers: a realization which encourages me to leave aside these theoretical considerations and go on to the interpretation of the works themselves, postponing these questions for another occasion yet not without the hope that some suggestions may arise—though obviously in a provisional and problematic form—out of these very "interpretations."

29

The Thonet chair exhibited in the Esprit Nouveau pavilion

## The furniture exhibited in 1929

Our point of departure for a detailed analysis of Le Corbusier's furniture (subsection, upright chairs and armchairs) is the furniture produced by Thonet. In describing the *Esprit Nouveau* pavilion in the 1925 Exhibition, Le Corbusier wrote: "We have chosen the humble chair by Thonet made of twisted beechwood, which is certainly the most economic of chairs, because I believe that this model, of which millions of examples are in use in the Continent and the two Americas, possesses a nobility of its own."[28]

Le Corbusier's adherence to the Thonet products is perfectly understandable when we remember that Michael Thonet (born in 1796) had invented the process of bending wood by means of steam (using fairly thin sections of wood), reduced the number of component pieces in articles of furniture, and taken the "decorative" form of the chairs out of their structure itself; in this way he had succeeded in producing articles of maximum solidity and economy, suited to the taste of the times and later to become classics. For these reasons there can be no question but that this furniture was the principal forerunner of modern design in this field. Compared with the millions of copies sold by the famous Viennese firm in all parts of the world, later output of mass-produced furniture, even when under the supervision of architects and designers, can be seen to be quite paltry. But of course the place of Thonet furniture in the history of design is more than quantitative. The quantitative success resulted from the almost unreserved approval granted by both the general public and the experts: all the qualities inherent in Thonet chairs were included in the program of the Modern Movement. As stated by Portoghesi, who rightly names the Viennese firm as one of the principal sources of art nouveau, "Even without proclaiming the fact, all modern architects who have handled the problem of interior design, from Rietveld to Breuer and Mies van der Rohe, have, wittingly or not, drawn on the invaluable heritage of Thonet."[29]

Certainly Le Corbusier himself was well aware of his debt, not only because the first edition of his set of furniture was produced by Thonet, but also because he may himself have had a direct part in the firm's production and adapted one of the most typical of Thonet armchairs to his own design. In fact, although I have found no confirmation of this in any book, it may well be the case that the model shown in the *Esprit Nouveau* pavilion was made by him. In this version, the back no longer consists of a double curve of bent wood in the shape of a horseshoe but is now a single piece incorporating the back legs and joined at the top edge by the arms made of one piece, like "bicycle handlebars." Not only this, but all the proportions of this small armchair have been modified: the seat has become a complete circle, the back lowered below the shoulders so as to lend greater support to the waist, while a double curve connects loosely the arms and this low back. We are now far removed from the taste of the nineteenth century and very close to the characteristics of purist painting and sculpture. If in fact Le Corbusier did not create this model, then it was a most extraordinary coincidence to find already in production an article of furniture so greatly congenial to his taste.

Besides, we find in some of Le Corbusier's armchairs a similar approach to that of Thonet. This has been described by Portoghesi: "The use of very few elements of construction, bent very freely, leads Thonet to a virtuosity which deforms the model he is imitating to the point of parody. Like a drawing made without lifting pen from paper, the technique creates problems, suggests a grammar and syntax, conditions the structure of the design."[30] In both the small and large versions of the "Fauteuil grand confort," in the structure of the chair and in particular the line of the front legs, bent once to contain the arms and again to contain the back, Le Corbusier seems to adopt the "technique" of never taking up his pen from the sheet on which he draws his design. But apart from this similarity, which may be a coincidence, corresponding moreover to a powerful critical interpretation, the debt owed by Le Corbusier to the ideas of Thonet goes further. To compare the most classic example of Thonet chairs with the chair by Le Corbusier just mentioned, substituting for the wooden circle the chrome-plated tubing (originally made of polished iron to keep costs down), and for the ring of the seat made of bamboo the horizontal supporting framework with its network of springs, in spite of the great divergence in form, we find ourselves in the presence of a scheme of construction of a similar type—a horizontal plane joined to vertical elements—whose rigidity is assured by a wooden ring in the case of Thonet, and a steel tube bent four times at an angle of 90° in the case of Le Corbusier. The main difference between these two models lies less in the different taste which informs them, the former following the "cult" of the line and the latter the dialectical interplay between line and volume, inspired by the maximum stereometry as required by the rationalist theory, than in the fact that the supporting and supported elements are blended in the one, whereas in the other the greatest possible emphasis is placed on their distinctiveness.

*Living room in the Esprit Nouveau pavilion, Paris, 1925. Sketch plan*

*Fauteuil grand confort (petit modèle), 1928. Version with steel chassis colored metallic grey-blue, cushions of leather and feathers. First edition*

Can one at this point rightly consider Le Corbusier's armchair a "sign"? And how shall we define a sign of this semeiotic system? We can say meanwhile that we shall not take the sign to indicate something which stands for something else, but as a form which encloses in its own particular shape the components of the sign which are, in linguistic terms, the well-known "signifying" and "signified" elements. Can we apply these terms to the object under discussion? The answer must be a decided affirmative, otherwise we cannot speak of a sign. The heart of the problem is to distinguish which part or which component in general of a design object is the "signifying," and which the "signified."

When on another occasion we considered the question of the semeiology of architecture, we defined the sign as the smallest unit endowed with internal space which can be exploited on a human scale (a room, for example). The components of this sign are the internal space taken as the "signified element" and the external space—the wall structure or at any rate the construction which envelopes this space—taken as the "signifying element."[31]

By reference to this type of sign, taken provisionally as a model for the semeiotics of design, and in the same way with the spatial factor taken as a basic yardstick for our entire argument, we can see how domestic objects, or household equipment, can be semeiotically classified and defined.

As a first classification, we can subdivide furniture into the groups of *containers* and *supports*, giving rise to two distinct systems of objects.

The whole range of containers, from the simplest basin to the most complex of partitioned cupboards, presents the basic opposition of inner/outer which in its turn produces a whole series of dichotomies: containing space/contained space, supporting/supported, concavity/convexity, etc. So that leaving aside the peculiar property of the architectural spatial sign, which represents an area to be exploited on a human scale, other container objects can be considered as signs as well, whose outer convex shape encloses an area of space, which is concave, and whose functional purpose is to hold liquids, solids or other objects. I believe the system of containers can be subdivided into sub-systems according to the characteristics of their various contents. The fact remains, however, that at least so far as their individual shapes are concerned, one may speak of the whole family of containers in terms of an exterior which is "signifying" and an interior which is "signified"—bearing in mind the differences which distinguish the language of architecture from that of design.

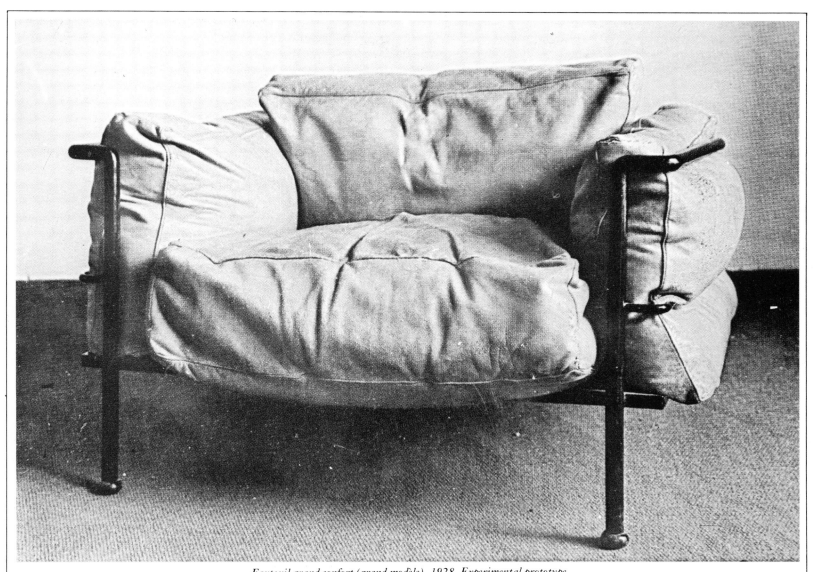

*Fauteuil grand confort (grand modèle), 1928. Experimental prototype*

It is a more complex question to define supporting objects. While the system of furniture which has a supportive function is entirely composed of articles proportional to the human scale, from bookcases to tables, from beds to seats, at the same time it consists of objects which differ not only in their function but also in the kind of relation they have to the human body. This gives rise to their different anthropometric forms and it is here that Le Corbusier conceived the idea of furniture as "human limb objects," for example. Thus one category might be a bookcase, another a table which must be of more exact anthropometric dimensions; one category a bed, which must not only be on human scale but possess further characteristics such as elasticity, softness, etc., while chairs, especially armchairs, represent another category since their shape envelopes the human body, sometimes to the extent that it resembles a negative impression of it.

For a more detailed classification of the supporting system of furniture, it would seem logical to examine it under these specific subheadings. But the point we have to reach is the answer to the question: What are the sign components of the object belonging to the system of supports—bookcases, tables, beds, upright chairs and armchairs?

Here many of the dichotomies which have been applied to container objects become partly or wholly invalid, and may all be reduced to the broad description of supporting/supported. This applies to all types of furniture classified in this system. But the real distinction between the design objects we have called containers and the supporting articles is spatial in nature. In the first group the components of the sign belong to the three-dimensional dominion of space, while in the second group they belong to a spatialism which is two-dimensional, built up on planes. Planes make up bookcases, tables, beds and even upright chairs and armchairs, and although these articles sometimes present an enveloping space, as has been said, this is always generated by a collection of planes and relates back to it. We can say therefore that the "signifying" component of a furniture-sign belonging to the system of supporting articles is provided by the part which acts as a support, while the "signified" component is provided by the supported part; the latter is often made up of one or more planes in direct contact with the human body, and these planes are obviously the reason for the existence of a similar type of furniture. At the outside, a bracket or the parts composing a very schematic chair—those by Rietveld for example—have a "signifying" aspect contrasting with the contact-surface which functions as a resting plane for man or the objects belonging to him, which we can define as the "signified"

*Fauteuil grand confort (petit modèle), 1928. Cassina, 1965*

element. In certain more complex versions the support supersedes in size and importance the part which it carries, but this does not alter the fact that it is the latter, even if no more than a simple plane surface, which is the reason for the existence of this article, that is, its "signified" element.

After this further theoretical digression, we can return to an analysis of Le Corbusier's furniture with new points of reference. We saw that in the "Fauteuil grand confort" considerable emphasis was placed on the distinction between the supporting part and the part which is supported, and for this reason it should probably be placed among the sign category of supports. But apart from this, one element is entirely external while the other is entirely internal and in direct contact with the human body it is intended to receive; one belongs to the realm of convexity, the other to concavity, etc. Such dichotomies, and especially the shape of the model, enable us to grasp the general meaning, or "message" of this sign object. Without of course neglecting its connotative aspects, that is, the "signified" elements which for one or another reason we associate mentally with the physical reality of this armchair, we can say that it expresses the logic of rationalism. This is seen in the paradoxical contrast between the enormous leather cushions and the apparently very slight supporting framework, and in the provision of maximum comfort with the minimum use of materials and labor, as is made possible by modern all-powerful technology. At the same time, both the slender and the massive components, which are kept continually in view so as to make the construction and "mechanism" of the chair completely explicit, are directed towards the ideal of proportion, commensurability and geometry—as befits the components of a single sign.

The influence of Thonet may again be seen in the "Chaise-longue à réglage continu." We are immediately reminded of the famous rocking chairs produced by the Viennese firm from the year 1860. The two models have in common the double tubing at the sides, which in the rocking chair serves both as a support for the seat and back and as a curved base to permit the rocking movement. In the "Chaise-longue," on the other hand, the upper section follows the anatomical shape of the sloping seat and back combined, which has been unified and enriched by a prolongation acting as a footrest (precedents for this solution can be considered the nineteenth century sofa and the models of reclining chairs with adjoining footrest), while the lower section forms a curve to allow for the various positions of the molded resting surface. Both chairs are in fact inspired by a particular dynamics: the

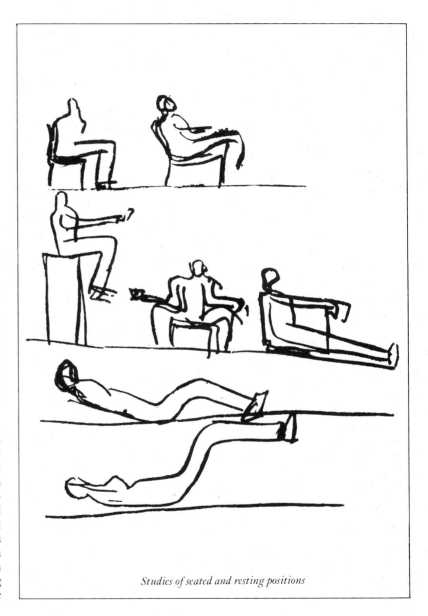

*Studies of seated and resting positions*

rocking chair establishes the body in a fixed position, leaving the rocking movement to the various slopes the chair produces; Le Corbusier too places the body in a fixed position, and in fact in a longer undulating anatomical surface, again permitting of various inclinations. The difference between these two chairs is that whereas in the rocking chair the different slopes are controlled by the person who remains seated, so rendering the chair unstable in a fixed position, in Le Corbusier's chair the angle has to be fixed before the sitter leans back, but in compensation for this limitation the chair remains firm in the chosen position once it has been selected.

In the case of this article of furniture, too, it does not seem to me relevant to speak of semeiotic dichotomies defining its "sign" nature, not even of its supporting/supported facets, the one classifiable as the "signifying," the other as the "signified" element; their dissimilarities are too great, and to some extent there is a degree of ambiguity in the steel support with boxlike metal section, the curved tube to control the chair's positions, and the molded chair surface. But the fact that it is difficult to apply some semeiotic dichotomies to the analysis of the object under discussion, even those found in any type of seat or armchair or bed—a supporting structure and a resting surface—does not necessarily invalidate this theoretical approach so much as it serves to indicate the actual limits of the object.

To add to what has been said regarding the significance of the "Chaise-longue" we note that just because of its originality and formal innovation it is the piece of furniture which presents the greatest problems of those designed by Le Corbusier. It seems to incorporate all the theory of rationalism: the use of new techniques, weightlessness combined with solidity, the juxtaposition of different kinds of material, and above all the concept of maximum functionalism. It can be said too that this chair is the literal embodiment of the view that household objects can be regarded as artificial limbs, or decorative art turned orthopedic. And it is true that this beautiful "resting machine," resembling a perfect Freudian analyst's couch, is almost unrecognizable as an article for use in the home, when seen without the presence of a person occupying it. And as if to make up for its distance from the traditional idea and shape of a chair, there is a quality of mimicry in it when seen perfectly in profile, copying the shape of the human body: it resembles a flaccid puppet with a round cushion in the place of a head. And in the conception of this model it does not seem irrelevant to remark on the play of words and ideas centered around the word "horse" (Fr. *cheval*). The leather of the seat is made of

36    *Thonet rocking chair, 1860*

pony, a trestle supports the whole chair (*chevalet*), while in their final version the legs are not unlike horses' hooves. With regard to the presence of someone to occupy the chair, it must be said that even in the Thonet chair, apart from the fact that we have been used to seeing it ever since the time of our grandparents, when seen without the presence of an occupant this rocking chair appears a very curious object. Both these chairs integrate perfectly with the person who occupies them, but whereas even the most ordinary version of the Vien-

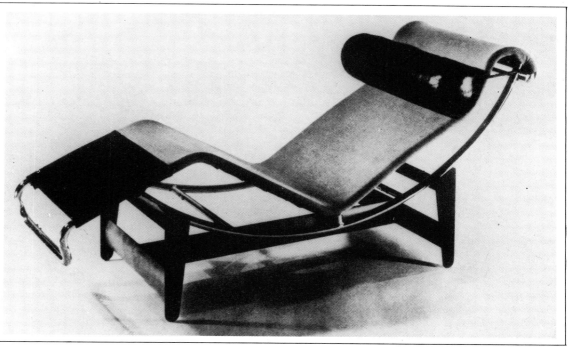

*Chaise-longue à réglage continu, 1928. Version with simplified supporting structure, without mesh support, covered in natural-color leather, cushion and footrest of natural leather. Prototype*

nese prototype immediately conveys a sense of relaxation as well as a note of bourgeois comfort, as might be expected in an article of furniture which has grown old with the home, Le Corbusier's "Chaise-longue à réglage continu" strikes one with its "scientific" severity, so that for many years this was one of the least popular pieces of contemporary design and had to wait a very long time before being industrially mass-produced.

Another piece shown in the 1929 group was the "Siège tournant," a

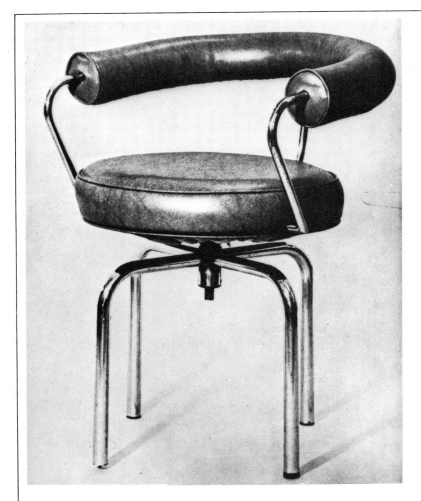

*Siège tournant (fauteuil), 1929*

*Siège tournant (tabouret), 1929*

padded stool with legs consisting of four steel tubes. This stool may be seen as the clearest exemplification of the theory that the supporting element should be kept as distinct as possible from the supported, taken by me as the two constituents of this type of furniture regarded as "signs." And this distinction, which is obvious in any kind of stool, is here given the particular emphasis which is consistent with according equal prominence and the same rigorous simplicity to both the supporting and the supported parts. In appearance at least, in order to avoid having another metal piece to connect the four tubes at their bottom end, though introducing a second horizontal line echoing the line of the padded seat, Le Corbusier considerably lowers the height of the legs by curving them outwards at a wide angle which both holds the seat rigid and connects with the swivel mechanism placed beneath its center; so that the massive volume of the cushion type of seat is placed over an "ideal" point, and from this same point the four metal tubes forming the legs begin, needing nothing to hold them together, thanks to their wide curve. The passage from the horizontal of the "signified" element to the vertical of the "signifying" is by way of a curve which, in its turn, ends in the swivel mechanism of the stool.

In the version of the "Siège tournant" with back, the intrusion of a feature which was undoubtedly out of balance led to a loss of logical rigor as found in the stool version, and here the resources of the figurative imagination came into being. The tubular back of padded leather is traversed right at its center by a metal tube attaching it to the seat, and slopes upwards at the back, in contrast to the perfect horizontality of the seat itself; it cannot be denied that this feature is a "deformation" of the original model. At the same time, however, since in the final analysis the result is highly valid, another component of Le Corbusier's design is revealed: the apparent obviousness of the solution recalls an *objet-trouvé*, or a certain spirit of *Je-m' en-foutisme*, in one respect close to the Dadaists as well as purist sculpture, and in another suggesting the idea of Le Corbusier as the initiator of brutalism.[32]

The adjustable table is another "sign" in which a sharp distinction is made between the "supporting" and "supported" elements. The former consists of two reversed U-shaped tubes—*tube d'avion à section ovoïde*—joined at the top center by a third ovoid tube section. A simple rectangular plane rests on this support held by four hinges to adjust the height of the table. The innovation in the use of new materials forms part of the intentions of the designer described earlier in

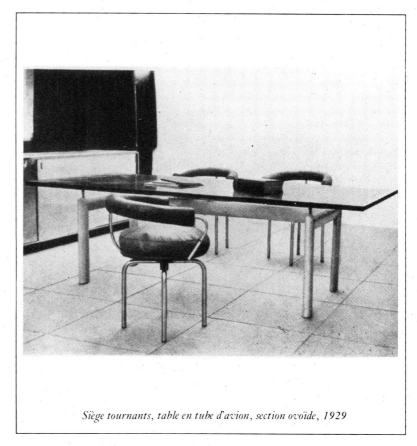

*Siège tournants, table en tube d'avion, section ovoïde, 1929*

this book; but apart from this and apart also from the hinges which not only serve to adjust the height but also to create distance, emphasizing the idea of keeping the carrying and carried elements distinct, is it still permissible, in spite of all this, to speak of two components of a single sign? I believe it is, even though here the "supporting" element is far more elaborate than the "supported," so that there is a lack of parity between the two components of the "sign." Indeed, with this particular support, and knowing Le Corbusier's interest in harmonic relationships, his careful preparatory sketches, and his idolatrous worship of proportion, I believe that no other type of supported element could be envisaged for this article of furniture. In other words, I think that this support could not have been used for anything other than this particular rectangular plane, taking into account the relation between the sides, its thickness, etc. If then this support is characterized by its lightness of weight associated to the maximum solidity, the same impression is conveyed by this solid linear plane which is held poised by bars at only four points. The significance of the whole "sign," as in other cases, lies entirely in this combination of massiveness and lightness.

We now come to the most significant piece in the whole group, the "Siège à dossier basculant." No longer is there any connection with the technique of Thonet, more precisely with the structural conception of the Viennese chairs (taken here as a paradigm for several other models). The constructive principle on which these chairs are based is the association of closed frameworks—one being the seat, another being formed at the chair-back by the curve of the circle of wood, while other closed frameworks keep the legs rigid and strengthen the back—and the only free-standing elements are the four legs. In this chair by Le Corbusier, in contrast, separate metal sections are used together, but none of them contributes to the formation of closed frameworks. Viewed from the front, side or rear, there are always three metal tubes, two vertical and the third horizontal, to form a letter H, with the single exception that from a side view the horizontal aspect of the third element is lacking, as will be discussed later. It is apparent that the firmness of the whole structure depends completely upon that of these metal tube sections, upon the strength of their joins, since they have to bear much pressure, and above all in the places at which the joins are sited. Some more detailed comment ought to be accorded to the siting of the points at which the tubes meet, and to the section of molded tubing at the side of the armchair, that is, the line which simultaneously fulfills a static and a functional role, supporting both the seat and the chair-back. We have seen that the front and back parts of the armchair each comprise two vertical bars and one horizontal bar; these vertical tubes are free-standing at the tops and bottoms with the result that the arms become reduced to two leather straps which play no part in connecting the sides of the chair together. This feature seems to have grown out of the designer's intuition of a static expression, since it is not supported by any scientific theory or constructive technique, and it is here that the key to the entire structure is revealed. The sides are connected to the front tubes at a point not far distant from where the crossbar of the front H is joined, on the same front tubing but on a plane in line with the side plane; from this meeting point, sloping at a given angle—that of the seat—is the side element, until it reaches the end of the seat; from here it bends at almost 90° then curves back to form a short rectilinear section which connects it to the rear tubing at right angles. This meeting point is sited almost at the top of the rear upright. The molding of the element just described and its joins make the structure so firm that it seems to have the strength of at least two parallel crossbars. But the characteristics of these two molded elements, one to each side, are not confined to this intelligent static function. They support the seat, a simple leather surface folded over the tubing and having a network of metal springs underneath, while in their curved section they contain two hinges to hold the sloping back. This back has the same features of leather and springs as the seat, but supported this time by a closed framework, the only one in the whole chair. To sum up, the "Siège à dossier basculant" is like a game of skill, as if Le Corbusier had made a wager that he could design an armchair using no more than eight pieces of tubing and create not only an admirable static equilibrium but a sense of great solidity—a result he could obtain only by making his chosen materials work to their maximum. The movement of the back confers the sense of a mechanism, which he inserted into his furniture whenever possible, but this effect is attenuated by his other criterion regarding the use of precious materials, as we find in the seat, the back and the arms, in other words those parts of this "machine" which are in contact with the human body.

In speaking of this metal armchair of Le Corbusier's, we are almost forced to make a comparison with the chair made a few years previously (1926) by Marcel Breuer and named "Wassilij," in homage to his old Bauhaus friend and colleague Kandinsky. At first sight the chairs are fairly similar and are expressive of a similar taste and style. In shape and structure both chairs reflect the belief that the supporting and supported elements no longer need to be sharply distinguished, but rather fused, especially in the Breuer. The main difference between them is that whereas Le Corbusier's chair, as has been said, rejects the use of a closed framework, in the Breuer chair the closed framework is the recurrent motif and basic constructive principle. In fact the support consists entirely of a single closed framework which by means of a single line curved several times encloses all four sides of the chair. To this basic structure the framework of the seat is attached, and the seat in turn rests upon another autonomous framework, that of the chair-back. A crossbar on each side holds these

*Table en tube d'avion, section ovoïde, 1929*
*Siège à dossier basculant, 1929*

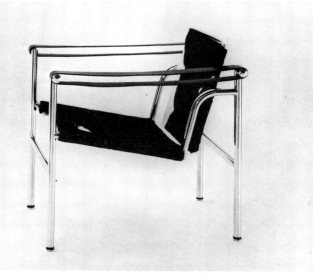

three elements rigid and fixes the point at which the chair-back framework slopes. Another considerable difference between these two chairs lies in the fact that whereas each section of metal tubing in the Le Corbusier is firmly welded to the next, in the Breuer all the joins—between one framework and another, as well as between the individual sections—are made by bolts, so that the elements of metal tubing present a sectional view. Again, while in the "Siège à dossier basculant" both the seat and back seem to be adapted to a pre-existent structure, even though they are imbued now with a sense of all parts being fused together, in the "Wassilij," on the other hand, because of their arrangement and the way they are connected, the different surfaces (originally made of strong canvas, later replaced by leather) themselves appear to have been the determining factors in deciding the moldings and various curves of the metal structure. To sum up, the German model contains a dialectical interplay of tubes and surfaces, or a figure in which the two diverse materials employed may be said to reverse their natural properties—the canvas or leather appearing rigid, the steel tubing seeming pliable—and in this way so unified an image is created that the diversity within it is eventually suppressed. Perhaps a weak point of this masterpiece of design of the 1920s is a degree of inflatedness: it creates an impression of superfluity, although this has the compensatory advantage that it confers a sense of richness and opulence to the armchair which goes beyond the limitations of the constructive program of the Bauhaus and even beyond their theory of design. In comparison with Le Corbusier's chair—which however it surpasses from several points of view, not least that of functionalism—the Breuer model may be termed "hyperstatic" in construction and "baroque" in style. And these thoughts suggest to us also the sense and meaning of the two models we are comparing. If we take as the archetype for both models Rietveld's "Red and Blue" chair of 1918, then Breuer's represents an "extension" of it while Le Corbusier's represents a "reduction."

*Notes*
[28] In "Almanach d'Architecture moderne," Paris, 1925, p. 145
[29] P. Portoghesi, *Thonet e la produzione di serie*, in "La botte e il violino," June 1964
[30] Ibid.
[31] Cf. R. De Fusco, *Segni, storia e progetto dell'architettura*, Laterza, Bari, 1971
[32] Cf. R. Banham, article "Brutalism," in *Enciclopedia dell'architettura moderna*, Garzanti, Milan, 1967, pp. 81–82

*Voisin Car, 1926*

## The historical background of Le Corbusier's furniture

In the preceding paragraphs we have examined Le Corbusier's opinions on the "decorative arts" and defined them as his theory of design. After our "reading" of the individual pieces shown in 1929 by means of an analysis of their forms and an interpretation of their significance as "signs," we go on to situate this period of Le Corbusier's production in its historical background. We must look at two aspects: on the one hand, the links with the culture, society, costume and fashion of the 1920s; on the other, the relationship existing between these pieces of furniture and others produced previously or contemporaneously, so showing the position they occupy internally within this sphere of production.

As for the first aspect, the accepted view of rationalism as an international tendency, the cosmopolitanism of Le Corbusier, and even his Swiss origin, have caused many historians and commentators to fail to notice the typically French element which permeates the whole of his work. It is rather surprising that they should have neglected to consider Le Corbusier as a forerunner who was ahead of his time and therefore always completely up to date, for when we see him in the photographs of the time he appears so very much at home in his period—beside his old friend Perret, in the portraits with Ozenfant, and above all with the women of the time, the vestals of fashion who provide what is probably the best index to the taste of a period. I believe indeed that it is quite helpful to our understanding of Le Corbusier, especially when we are considering the more "frivolous" sphere of furnishings for the home, to think of his furniture in the presence of girls dressed *à la garçonne*, or young men wearing Zouave trousers, the style of dress worn mainly by the American colony in Paris, whose names alone suffice to recall the whole climate of an epoch.

The most recent description we have of the Paris of the 1920s can be found in the attractive, well-informed pages of someone who herself participated in these events, Giulia Veronesi, who will surely remain unsurpassed among contemporary art historians for her account of the cultural background in the Vienna of Olbrich and Hoffman, the Milan of Persico and Pagano, and other great European cities in the book to which I refer, entitled *Stile 1925, ascesa e caduta delle "Arts Déco" (Style 1925, the Rise and Fall of the Decorative Arts).*

In this book the writer speaks of a Paris where all interests, from the most austere to the most self-indulgent, were blended into a unified whole. In relation to the general direction of French culture in the 1920s, we read that it was "marked by cubism but still linked to the 'decantation' of a far-off Parnassian spirit, which kept it in the direction of paradox all the time, measuring its 'sur-realism' and openmindedness against a regulating factor of a rationalist type, and in an extremely elegant and revitalizing 'line of irony'."[33]

In defining some details of that cultural background, Veronesi offers us an example of her ability to bring together the apparently most heterogeneous elements, and this merits a textual quotation. In a comparison of the Ballets Russes of Diaghilev in the pre-war period with the post-war "bals-nègres," which in their turn were related to African sculpture, a source of inspiration to Picasso, Modigliani and many other artists, and to American jazz, she writes: "Paris flocked to the first 'bals nègres,' jazz gradually took the place of the gypsy violin and the Charleston replaced the tango: even before Josephine, the amazing twenty-year-old mulatto, came to complete the picture in 1925. . . . And, once again, the whole 'decorative' aspect of Parisian life and art was affected, starting with fashion, which since the war had been modeling itself on the figure of the *garçonne.* . . . The young girls had been called up for war work and had been dressed in a plain dress and jacket, or *tailleur* with the skirt above calf length, but once they became idle this skirt was widened into a bell shape and given the name *crinoline de guerre*; and when the war was over Gabrielle Chanel, nicknamed Coco, adopted the doctrine of simplicity and began to put dread into the tailor of luxury Poiret, just as with his cubic houses the architect Mallet-Stevens began to put dread into Perret, the architect who was the favorite of the upper middle class."[34]

I have made reference to the American colony in Paris. Paris (one might equally say Europe) and America represented two opposed camps and the intellectuals of the two continents observed the scene from contrasting viewpoints. The Europeans, and foremost among them possibly architects, from Loos to Le Corbusier, looked to America as a model of everything which is pragmatic and efficient to set against their misunderstood sense of the European tradition. In contrast the Americans were disillusioned by the very qualities which evoked the admiration of their European counterparts, and came to the heart of the old continent of Europe to look for the sense of individuality, which, whether because of its history, its society of varied personalities or its *avant-garde* experimentalism, characterized the Paris of the period. Whatever the reason which drew them there, at the time when Le Corbusier was a young man Paris had an American

43

*Notes*

[33] G. Veronesi, *Stile 1925, ascesa e caduta delle "Arts Déco,"* pub. Vallecchi, Florence, 1966, p. 78

[34] Ibid., p. 82

[35] For an over-all view of the principal chair models from the nineteenth century until today, see the article *S'asseoir '74,* concerning an exhibition held in Grenoble Museum from June to October 1974, in the journal *Domus,* No. 538, September 1974.

[36] E. Persico, *Ruhlmann,* in "Tutte le Ópere (1923–1935)," Edizioni di Comunità, Milan, 1964, pp. 172–3.

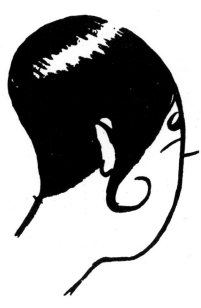

*On these pages, pictures of Josephine Baker*

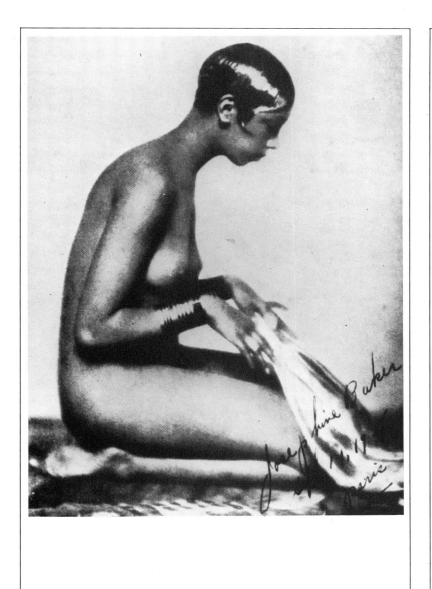

*Pencil sketch by Amadeo Modigliani, 1914*

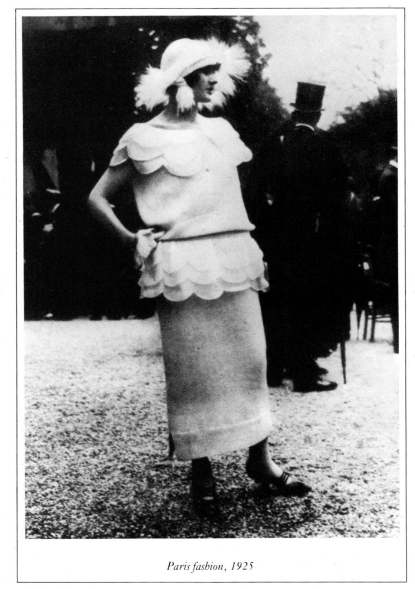

*Paris fashion, 1925*

*Poster by Georges Lepape for the tailor Poiret, 1920. Lithograph*

46

colony founded by Leo Stein with his sister Gertrude and with Ezra Pound, and was the temporary or permanent home of the best American artists, including Hemingway, Scott Fitzgerald, Dos Passos, Sherwood Anderson, Sinclair Lewis, Henry Miller, Thornton Wilder and the Dadaist photographer Man Ray.

To pass from these background notes to the "precedents" which in the sector of furniture for the home may be associated with the furniture of Le Corbusier, we find apart from the Thonet production some armchairs designed by Hoffman, in particular his "Purkersdorf," dated 1903, "Armlöffel," 1908, and "Kubus," 1910, which even in name precedes Le Corbusier's two versions of the "Fauteuil grand confort," commonly known as the "cube." Other models which preceded Le Corbusier's, especially his "Siège, à dossier basculant," are Rietveld's armchair "Red and Blue," dated 1918, as previously mentioned, the Breuer chair of 1925 which preceded the "Wassilij," the "Chair without end" of 1926 by Mart Stam, and the chair by Mies van der Rohe called "256," also dated 1926. Contemporary with Le Corbusier's armchairs are Breuer's "Cesca" of 1928 and "S35L" of 1929, and the famous Mies van der Rohe "Barcelona" armchair designed in 1929 also for the German pavilion in the Exhibition organized in the city of that name.[35]

But while the models just referred to may be associated with those by Le Corbusier through their technique of construction, their stylistic orientation, and their exemplification of the rationalist code they held in common, it must not be overlooked that more than one tie binds them to precedents which are typically French; it does not matter that these were still the expression of excellent craftsmanship, the unique example, and a luxury market. We recall particularly the work of Jacques-Emile Ruhlmann, whose extremely refined furniture combined geometric simplicity with the juxtaposition of such precious materials as ebony and ivory and whose liking for furniture composed of broad masses supported by very slender mounts brought him close to Le Corbusier. In addition to these formal aspects, there are other links, though indirect, which relate this highly prized French designer to Le Corbusier. Ruhlmann used to say: "Fashion does not come from below, and it is expensive to create. To start with the cheap article of furniture in mind is a heresy, because the luxury article then becomes the champion of current production." As is seen, this program was at the opposite extreme from the rationalist theory and was stigmatized because of this in the 1930s. However, one writer who was able to see beyond the ideas of the critics of his time was

*Coco Chanel*

Persico, and he established the affinity between Ruhlmann and Le Corbusier on the basis of this predilection for richness, which he saw as a phenomenon to be encountered even in modern design. He wrote in this connection, "What does it matter if Ruhlmann is the French bourgeoisie, and the others the *avant-garde?* 'Ruhlmann [we read in a recent *tableau* by Colombier and Manuel], exigent to excess as regards the quality of what he produces, has worked only for a very rich clientele, for whom he has alternatively supplied models which are too sumptuous, encrusted with ivory, and extremely simple models where, in our view, he shows his refinement more clearly.' I shall speak well of both here: without being shocked at their ornateness as of a bad example, without taking too much notice of the fact that these 'models' of Ruhlmann's, together with those of Süe and Mare, came to represent the 'Victoire' style, with its taste for the over-elaborate. Perhaps the style of Le Corbusier—a metal armchair, an adjustable table, a surrealistic carpet—is of a different type? If we look closely, there is but one difference; Ruhlmann was the *ensemblier* of the French bourgeoisie; Le Corbusier is preparing to be the same for the bourgeoisie of all Europe."[36] As can be seen, all we were seeking was a precedent of style or costume, but we have found what is the nodal point of design and its failure, at least so far, as an art accessible to everyone.

47

## Le Corbusier's furniture today

It has been authoritatively stated that the majority of the pieces exhibited in 1929 have since become classics. In the words of Rogers: "Objects become antiques when they have gone past the stage of being old, but this is a quality possessed by only a few choice examples. Once they have become antique, they again form part of the patrimony of the day and we can make practical use of them in our daily culture. Le Corbusier . . . is always modern in every object he produces, because there is no urban design, no individual building, no piece of furniture, which, while expressing the time when it was conceived, does not transcend it to form part of a universal patrimony. A chair by Le Corbusier is as valid as a Savonarola, or the Barcelona Chair by Mies van der Rohe, or the furniture of Thonet, in short, as those few objects among so many which have existed whose age may be measured in centuries or decades, yet belong to all time."[37]

I myself am broadly in agreement with this opinion and believe it explains why Le Corbusier's furniture is still up to date. But it should not be overlooked that this view is essentially based on aesthetic considerations and that these do not fully embrace every aspect of design.

There is no doubt that Le Corbusier's furniture is much more up to date and significant than the innumerable models produced today to fit in with a very tame kind of "pop-Dadaism" in comparison with what might have been (we recall the example of Kurt Schwitters), or with the supertechnology which is reduced to filling plastic molds, even imitating the old "Frau" armchairs, or to "reproduce"—and this is the most widespread tendency—car seats for household furniture. If all this is true, however, how can anyone still register shock at furniture which employs steel tubes in place of wood? And is there still something surprising in the adoption of metal sections such as are used in airplane construction? What I am saying is that many of the controversial ideas associated with Le Corbusier's furniture, having had the function of contesting a particular mode, fashion or method of manufacture, have in theory won their battle, and now that we can see the extent to which they were directed to the overthrow of that order, they undoubtedly show signs of age. So that if the justification and "signified element" of these articles of furniture had been limited to these polemics, we should have had to deduce that in form too they had aged. In actual fact this is not always the case. While the

*J. E. Ruhlmann: furniture made of macassar wood and ivory, 1925*

48

mechanically inspired model played a considerable part, as we saw when discussing the theory of Le Corbusier, there exists in these models a margin of multivalency which supersedes their mechanical aspect and even the fashion of the period (for example, that sense which makes the fashion of the period appear ridiculous to us although we value it as an indicator of taste) and it is this quality which allows them to become antique after having been old, or in other words turns them into classics. But even when we say this, we still remain in the ambit of an aesthetic argument, omitting two questions which seem to be of paramount importance in a consideration of design.

The first of these is broadly semeiological in character and leads to the stating of a problem rather than to its solution. Since design, to use the criteria of Le Corbusier himself (or as he called it, though reluctant to employ this term, "decorative art") does not aim to produce works of art but objects which, although in line with a certain taste, are valid mainly because of their function and connotative values, which of these values have replaced the mechanically inspired aspects that today, to use a journalistic term, no longer make news?

First of all I would say, at least so far as the studies of experts are concerned, that the new connotative values are to be recognized by means of the operation of rediscovering "history," which is being undertaken in one way or another in architecture and closely allied fields. Objective tribute should be paid to the Cassina Company and its "collection of the Masters" of the Modern Movement and their precursors; although this is a commercial venture, it uses the best qualified experts in contemporary art history. As is known, their research attempts to look at the entire cultural heritage of the past, not so much for the messages contained in the works, or even their form and style (this would have been no more than a simple revival), but above all in order to re-examine the works of the past in their relationship to society, their methodology of planning and construction, and their structures. In other words, the heritage of the past is not searched for the *parole*/message today, but for the *langue*/code or structure. Moreover, since this concerns a "mechanism" which is internal to the language of architecture, even though the phenomena of the period are not ignored, these acquire a secondary importance, and it is for this reason that the researcher is free to observe one or another period and—because he seeks for a procedure which has remained almost constant through time, which is, we repeat, "internal" to the architectural phenomenon itself—he remains free from any fallacy of an

*A. Laprade: pavilion of the Grands Magasins du Louvre at the International Exhibition in Paris, 1925*

*L. H. Boileau: pavilion of the "Au Bon Marché" store at the International Exhibition, Paris, 1925*

eclectic type. A further safeguard from this risk of fallacy derives from the fact that modern technology and the contemporary demand for quantity transform these references to the past to such an extent that they transform them, making them, unlike eclecticism, unrecognizable as such and definable only in the sense of "quotations." Besides an interest in the past as it is generally understood, there exists too an interest in a past which is much more clearly defined and which has been felicitously termed "the tradition of the new," that is, the tradition of the Modern Movement. And to look into the tradition of the new means to see afresh and even re-create, with or without modifications (more will be said on this point later on), works of architecture, objects, entire movements, which for one reason or another did not have the opportunity to develop fully in their own time. This is true, for example, of the geometric tendency in art nouveau, which was overshadowed by the predilection for concave/convex forms, and in this connection Alison's study of the chairs of Mackintosh,[38] the greatest exponent of the first trend, is particularly relevant. It is true of the school of Amsterdam, overshadowed in its turn by the success of De Stijl; it is true of Expressionism, obscured by the rationalist movement. It is even true of the rationalist works which were not taken up sufficiently by the industrial production of the time: Rogers speaks of this in reference to a period of aging for the furniture of Le Corbusier, who for his own part wrote in those years: "On cherche une industrie qui se chargerait de réaliser des casier en grand série, sur format standard."

So that, to return to today, the new connotations which came to take the place of the mechanical ones were concerned firstly with the rediscovery of history and are valid as an affirmation against a present in which many, rightly or wrongly, are not recognized. In the second place, the sense of the duration of these pieces, their ability to seem up to date after more than forty years, imparts a connotation of stability and a guarantee of value, especially when we think of the often unjustified proliferation of so many new models. Not least among the other connotative aspects of this furniture is that it is valid for a whole generation of cultured users, as a testimony to their culture and their period, a period moreover spanning the inter-war years with all its limitations and undoubted victories. In other words, these pieces of furniture belong to the generation of our parents, a generation which was still effective as a ruling class, "against" their children's differently orientated generation. The fact that in spite of this our parents' generation did not feel that it was represented by the style of

50

*Erich von Stroheim, 1927*

*Ettore Petrolini in "Gastone"*

Le Corbusier, whereas their children do, is due to a lack of information and, one might say, the gap of a generation, which concerns us here only marginally.

Much more could be said on the subject of the connotative changes affecting the 1929 group of furniture by Le Corbusier, but I leave this aside now to pass on to the second question, which is prompted by the present-day production of this furniture group but is generally applicable to analogous aspects of design.

The question may be stated thus: without departing from the premise stated by Le Corbusier himself, that the design object aspires only in part to the condition of universality and immortality of the work of art, should one not perhaps more appropriately think of that object as something to be transformed through course of time, to reflect the changes in its use, its connotative significance, and hence even its form if it reveals defects—possibly of a technical nature—which ought to be put right?

In other words, in the sector with which we are concerned here, and which is involved in so many aspects of this question, would it not be more appropriate to aim at the continual perfecting of a few prototypes rather than the production of more and more completely new models, as is the case for works of art such as paintings and sculptures?

We do not, of course, overlook the fact that the proliferation of different models is due to the laws of supply and demand, in which are to be included the public's desire for novelty, the manufacturers' interest in putting more and more new goods on the market to take the place of those already there, the logic of induced needs, the demands of productivity, consumerism, etc. But while it would be absurd to disregard these factors which represent the motivation of industrial production, I believe that in addition to them the question just stated—that is, whether it would be preferable to keep perfecting a small number of prototypes rather than producing more and more new ones which must inevitably be imperfect—encounters some difficulty even at the level of theory and of the best qualified constructive production. Yet what has occurred in other sectors ought to substantiate the former hypothesis. We are reminded in particular of the many modifications brought to the famous Volkswagen model, without however fundamentally changing its original structure or character, or the more considerable modifications brought to the Citroën 2 CV, to which, as has been said, Le Corbusier himself contributed. If cars reflect the logic of consumerism and changes in

51

*Automobile show, Paris, 1925*

taste far more tangibly and noticeably, it is equally true that the sectors of design which are closest to architecture generally undergo a much slower transformation. But this is not the point: our aim is to discuss the legitimacy or otherwise of varying one single prototype, not to compare the different sectors of design from the viewpoint of their contemporaneity.

To confine our inquiry to the realm of furniture, there are further points to be considered. When we speak of the Savonarola or the Thonet, which prototype exactly do we have in mind? Usually we are not thinking of any one in particular, but rather of a certain method, an expression of taste, the result of a technique; in a word, we are not thinking so much of any specific form as principally of a "structure."

It should also be borne in mind that many of the criticisms which are still leveled at some sectors of design, especially that of furniture

and objects of domestic use, are founded on a theoretical attitude as well as on difficulties associated with commercial technology: more precisely, they are founded on an error of an aesthetic type. This consists in considering design objects as part of the sphere of art, that is, of unique and unrepeatable phenomena (we are not referring here to the mere multiplication of a prototype which, now universally accepted, detracts in no way from the aesthetic validity of the product), instead of as part of the realm of taste, of a general artistic attitude, with the movement from one to the other category—individualized in his way by Le Corbusier himself—occurring only exceptionally.

So that, in the case of Le Corbusier's furniture—but this argument may be applied more generally, when we are confronted with the revival of "historical" models—we can formulate some hypotheses on the meaning of this revival.

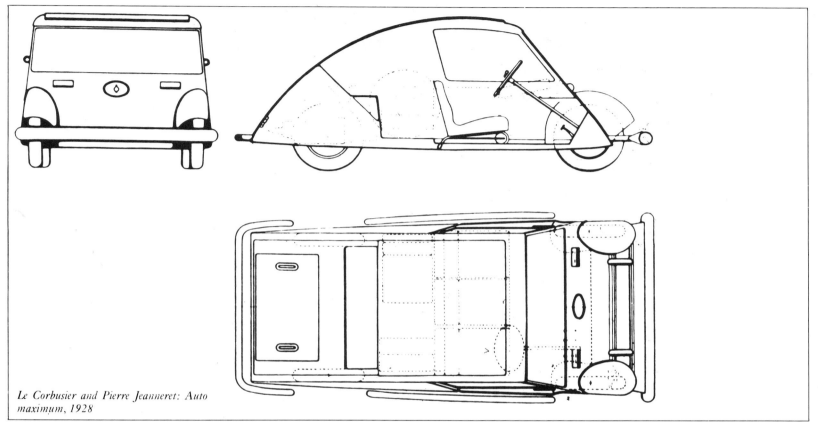

*Le Corbusier and Pierre Jeanneret: Auto maximum, 1928*

In the first place, because of their creator's prestige, because they are paradigmatic works serving as models for later modifications, because they are rich in denotative and connotative significance, they could be considered as phenomena of a prevailingly expressive and artistic character, which enabled them to become antique after a period of aging and to be put forward again just as they were first conceived.

The second hypothesis is to consider such furniture as not having aged because it is susceptible to continuous modification, not so much as the result of a "patient research" as especially a manifestation of a process still going on, as in the case of such objects as cars, office ma-

chinery, precision tools, etc., restoring to them that "noble" sense of anonymity which pertains to the very life of design and in general to the products of an old but dynamic expression of culture.

Both these solutions have some validity and justification; and one cannot exclude the fact that even the "static" conception, which in the first hypothesis corresponds to the "aesthetic" conception of design, can in its way admit of transformations and updating on the basis of the concept of the "open-ended work." If we had to choose between the two hypotheses stated above, I believe that because some modifications to these "historic" pieces have inevitably been effected, and in view of what Le Corbusier himself wrote on the dynamic process of

Notes
[37]E. N. Rogers, in *Le Corbusier e il "Design" moderno*, in the monograph quoted
[38]Cf. F. Alison, *Le Sedie di Charles Rennie Mackintosh*, Documenti di Casabella/Warehouse Publications, Segrate, 1973

*Above: Gerrit Rietveld, Red and Blue Chair, 1918*
*Above right: Ludwig Mies van der Rohe: Chair and table, 1927*
*Below: Le Corbusier: Maison La Roche, Paris. Interior, as it is today*
*On page 55, above: Marcel Breuer: dining room, 1926*
*Below: Robert Mallet-Stevens: office furniture, 1928*

industrial civilization, there are many reasons for taking seriously the second way and choosing the hypothesis of *work in progress*, the perfectible life of the forms of the furniture which has been examined.

But on a closer view the present-day industrial production of some of the "historic" works of the Masters can be said to supersede the two suggested hypotheses, which have been stated here in order to clarify our ideas and to serve as a point of reference.

For if it can be said that the first hypothesis supports the "aesthetic" viewpoint while the second favors the "practical," the historical operation of reviving works of the Masters presents its own justification in that it favors a "cultural" movement, and we can take this as a third hypothesis relative to the problem with which we are concerned.

To revive today the works of Mackintosh, Rietveld, Le Corbusier, etc., is to come right into the movement of historical revival which has been referred to in the preceding pages. Its principal value is as a critical reply to the production of today; as a rediscovery of qualities which remained either unexplored or incompletely developed; and in particular as a "projectual" phenomenon. While being, as such, a movement carried out from the top, by experts in the field, it is prompted by more general considerations: a need for reassurance, a desire to avoid further waste of talent, a wish to counteract the tendency towards the transient fashions and vicious circle of consumerism. So that far from being a nostalgic activity, an escape from the present or an eclectic revival, the return to the works of the Masters, with the critical and historical research that accompanies it, is one of the most tangible aspects of present-day architectonic research into the new relationship between the works of the past and plans for the future. In the phenomenology of this relationship, in which we are all engaged in one way or another, the first term loses every aura and aestheticism to enter the "operative" field, while the second term loses every fanciful claim to modify reality and plan for the new developments without reference to any precedent or code of theory.

If by history we mean contemporary history, or an activity envisaged according to the needs of today, and if planning is an activity involving constructing according to a model, the most reliable being the historical model, then no one can fail to see that the possibility of, so to speak, projecting history and historicizing planning not only forms a unified operation but one which is perhaps the most reasonable possible in the present highly uncertain stage of culture.

55

**Models and Production**

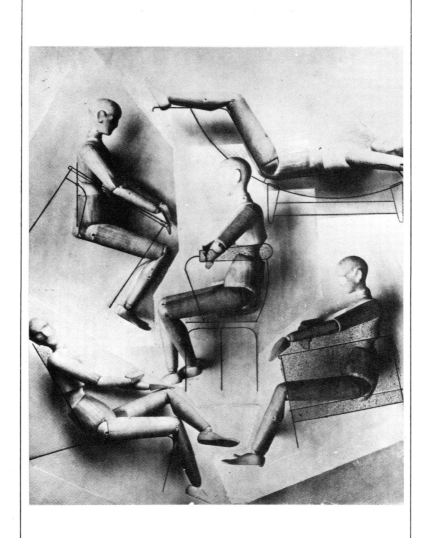

*Studies of body positions using a lay-figure, 1928*

*Catalogue of the metal furniture designed by Le Corbusier, Pierre Jeanneret and Charlotte Perriand (the designers' initials appear at the side of each sketch)*

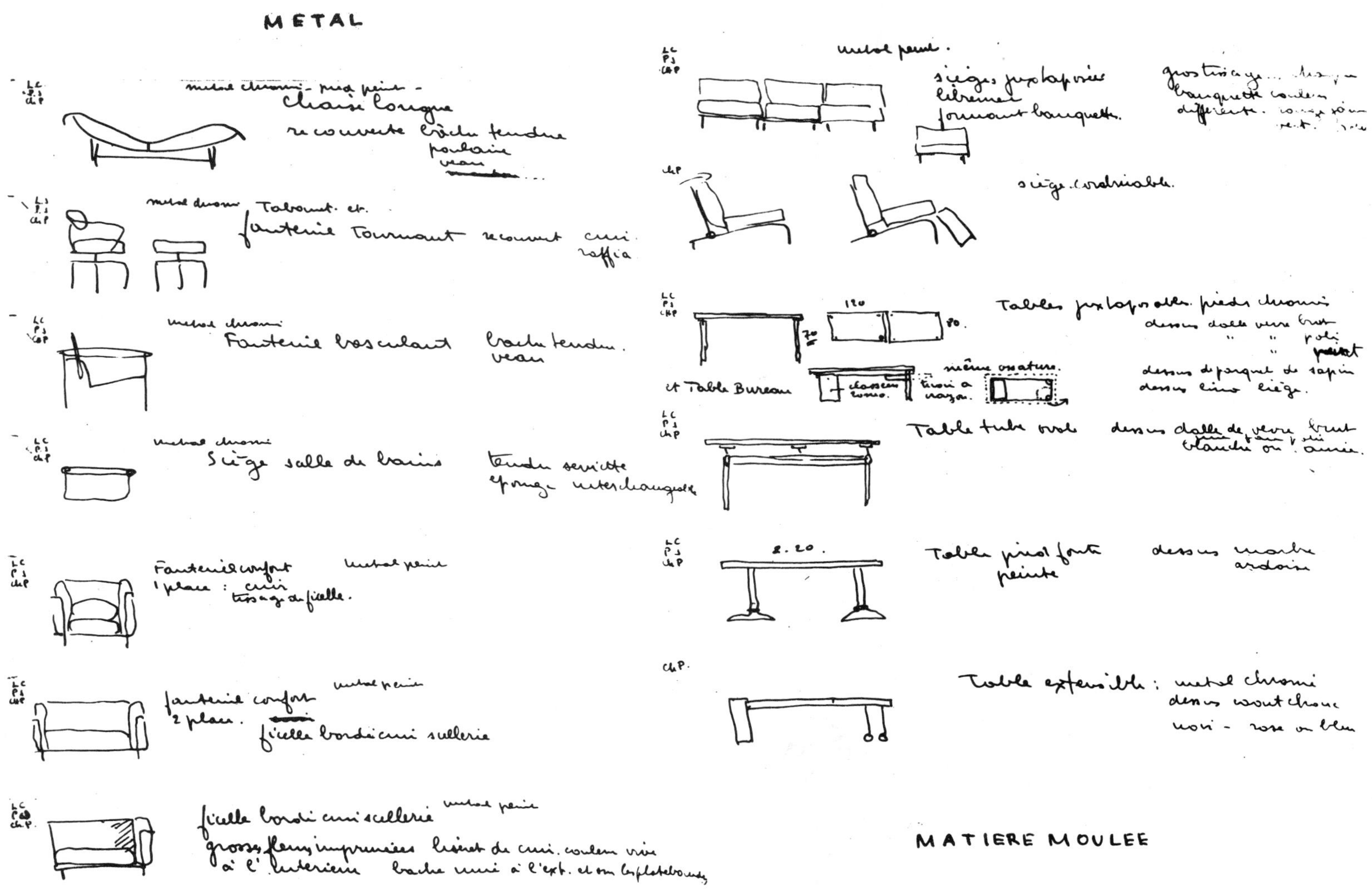

Equipement intérieur d'une habitation, Salon d'Automne, Paris, 1929

Le Corbusier, Pierre Jeanneret, Charlotte Perriand .

**1 Siège à dossier basculant, 1929**
(64 x 60 x 65cm)

Production: Thonet, 1928; H. Weber, 1959; Cassina, 1965

Support of polished or nickel-plated steel tubing, seat and back of leather or pony
This is the most significant piece of the whole group, and unlike the other models is made by putting together a number of metal sections, none of which contributes to the formation of closed frameworks.
The rocking back makes for a restful posture throughout all its positions. The arms are two continuous leather straps which rotate freely round the two ends of the uprights.
In its shape, its mobile back and the strap-arms, this chair is inspired by the "Safari" chair, used previously by Le Corbusier in some of his interiors.
The modulated cube geometry which it encompasses and the knobs on the uprights recall the image of the faldstool.

*1, 2. Version with framework in polished steel tubing and pony skin. Cassina Production, 1974*
*3. Version in satinated steel and canvas, 1929*
*4. Version in satinated steel and pony skin, 1929*

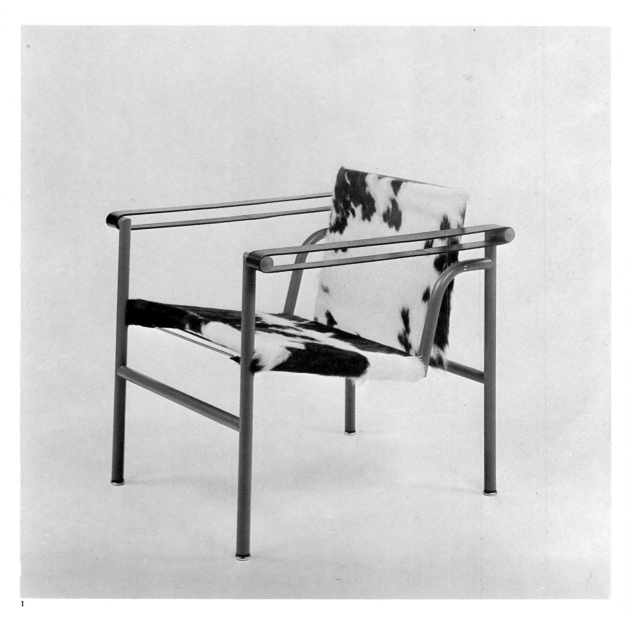

1

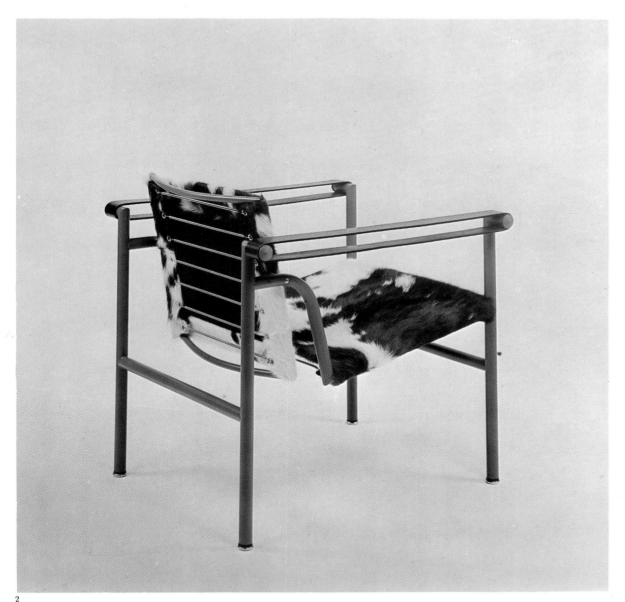

2

3, 4

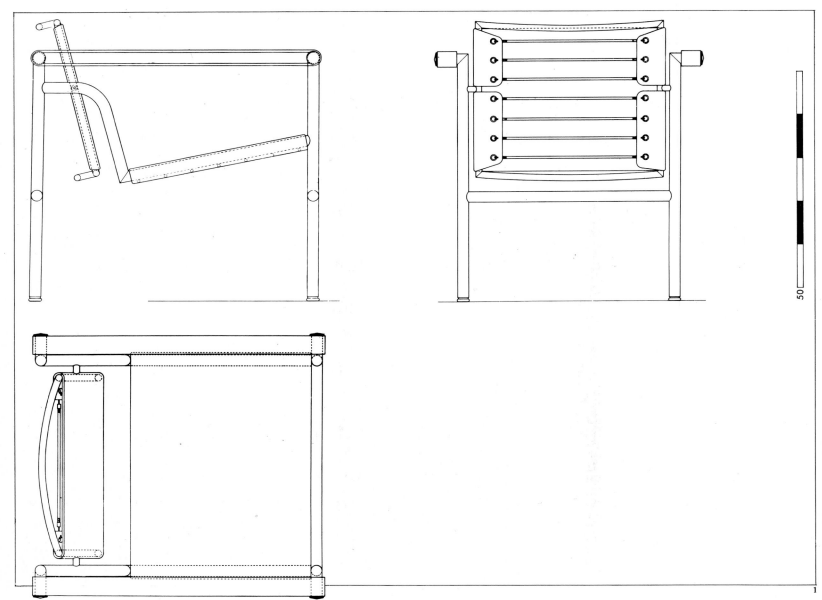

50

*Siège à dossier basculant:*
1. Working drawings of the present-day production
2. Hall of the Swiss Pavilion of the Cité Universitaire, Paris, 1932
3. Version in wood and straw by Charlotte Perriand for a young man's apartment at the Brussels International Exhibition, 1935
4. Version in satinated steel and leather, 1929

2

3, 4

Equipement intérieur d'une habitation, Salon d'Automne, Paris, 1929

Le Corbusier, Pierre Jeanneret, Charlotte Perriand

**2 Fauteuil grand confort, Petit modèle, 1928**
(67 x 76 x 70 cm)

**3 Fauteuil grand confort, Grand modèle, 1928**
(62 x 99 x 68 cm)

Production: Thonet, 1928; H. Weber, 1959; Cassina, 1965

A group of cushions placed side by side into a cage of chrome-plated or polished steel tubing grey-blue in color.
Emphasis is placed on the distinction between supporting and supported structure, the one entirely external, the other internal; one belongs to the reign of convexity, the other to that of concavity.
They express the logic of rationalism: the paradoxical contrast between the enormous leather cushions and their apparently very slight support; the maximum of "confort" with the minimum use of materials and "toil."

*Fauteuil grand confort, grand modèle:*
*1. Version in polished steel with fabric-covered cushions. Cassina, 1974*
*2, 3. Version in nickel-plated steel with leather-covered cushions. Cassina, 1965*

62

1

2

3

*Fauteuil grand confort, petit modèle:*
*1, 2, 3. Version in nickel-plated steel*
*with leather-covered cushions. Cassina,*
64    *1965*

1

2

3

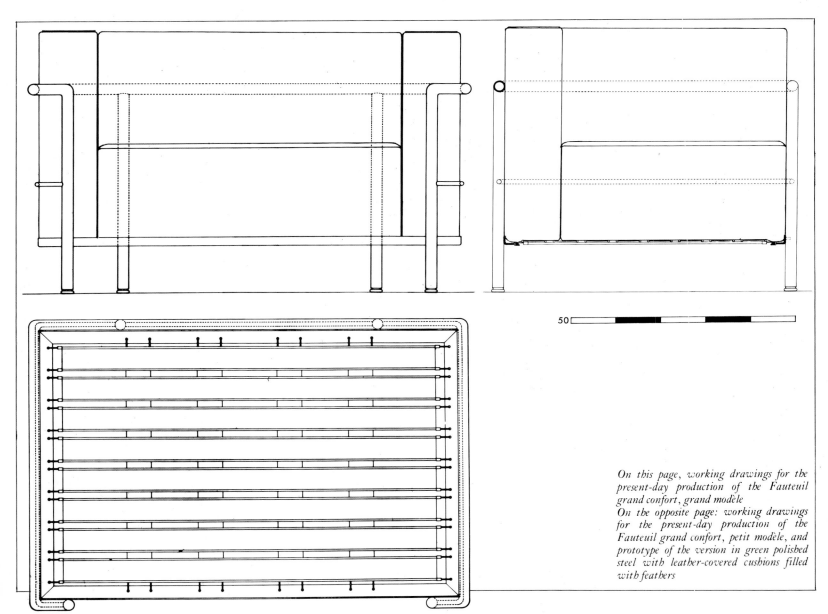

On this page, working drawings for the present-day production of the *Fauteuil grand confort, grand modèle*
On the opposite page: working drawings for the present-day production of the *Fauteuil grand confort, petit modèle*, and prototype of the version in green polished steel with leather-covered cushions filled with feathers

50

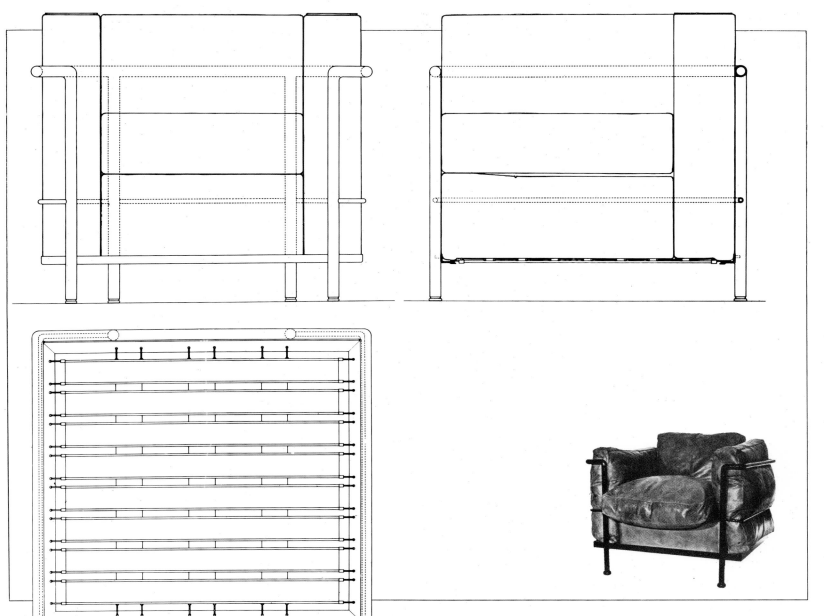

Equipement intérieur d'une habitation, Salon d'Automne, Paris, 1929

Le Corbusier, Pierre Jeanneret, Charlotte Perriand

**4 Chaise-longue à réglage continu, 1928**
(60 max. x 57 x 160 cm)

Production: Thonet, 1928; H. Weber, 1959; Cassina, 1965

The upper structure, of chrome-plated or polished grey-blue steel, rests on a greyish iron trestle.
The broken line of the moulded seat forms a very elegant contrast with the broad curve upon which it rests and is adapted to support the body in repose. This model carries out to the letter the theory that objects of design can be viewed as artificial limbs, that is, decorative art which has become orthopedic.
From any angle the stability of the seat is assured by the friction of the rubber tubes which cover the crossbars of the support.
In this object the entire concept of rationalism is embodied: the new technology, the sense of lightness combined with solidity, the juxtaposition of diverse materials, but above all the ideal of maximum functionalism.

*1. Version in nickel-plated steel. Cassina, 1965*
*2. Version in polished steel. Cassina, 1974*

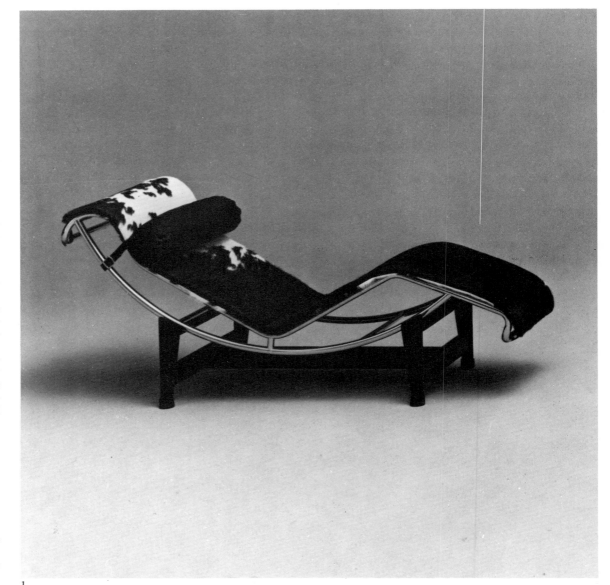

1

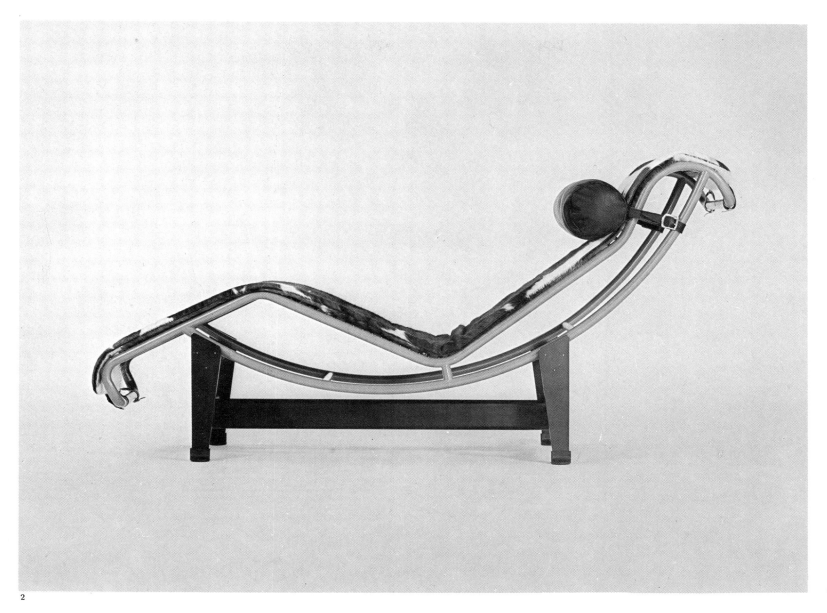

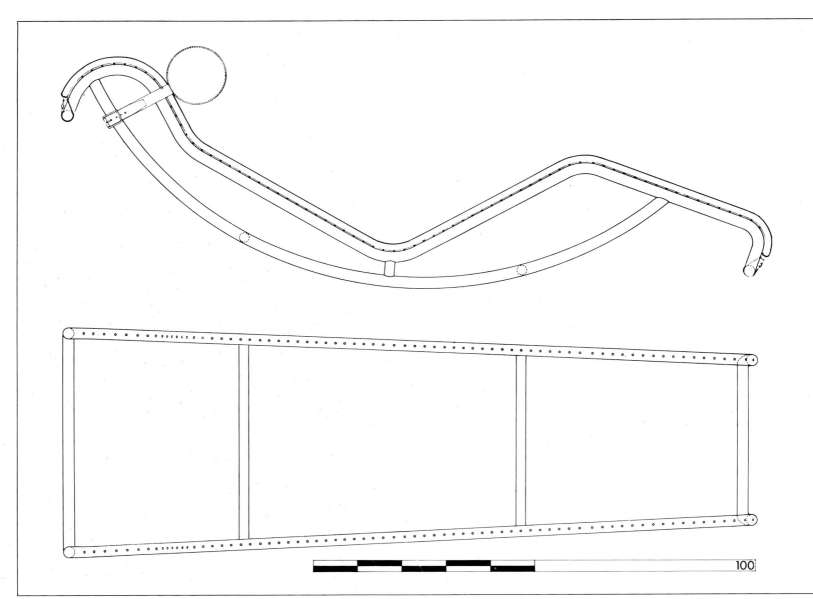

100

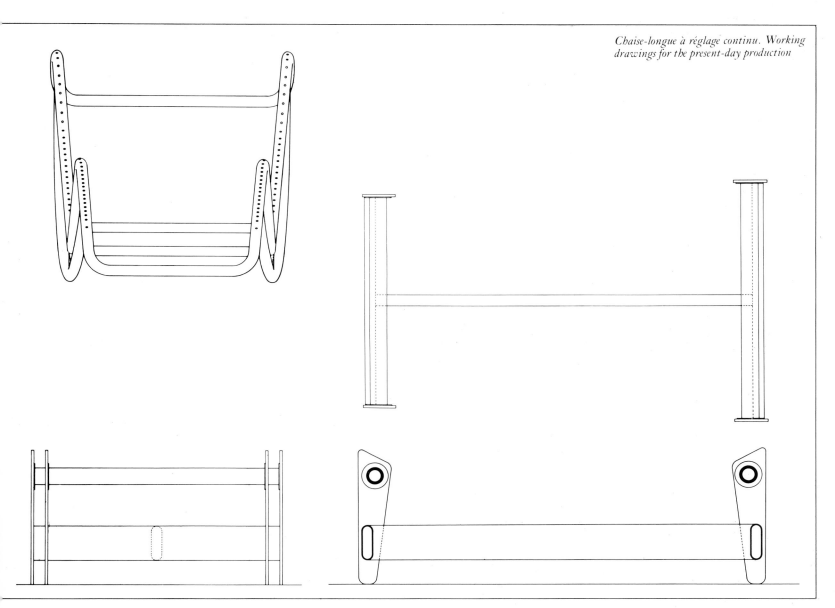

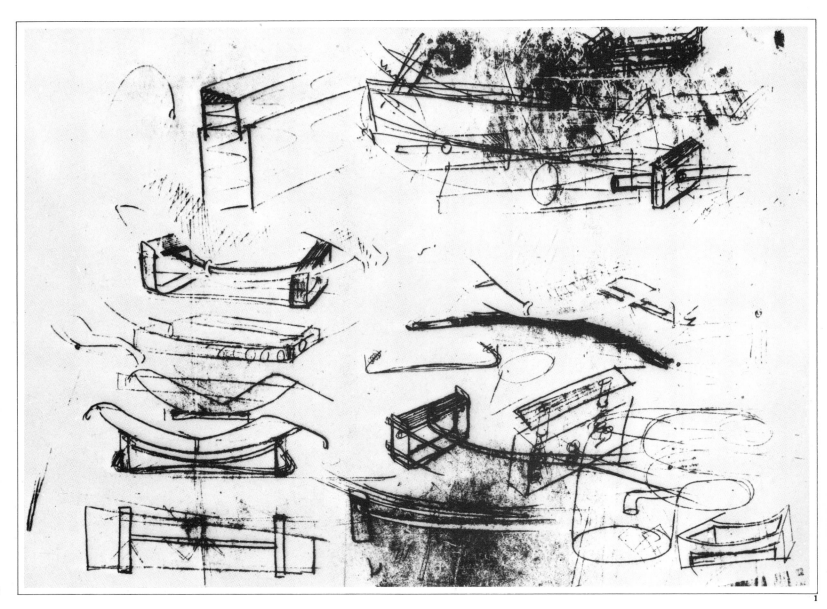

72

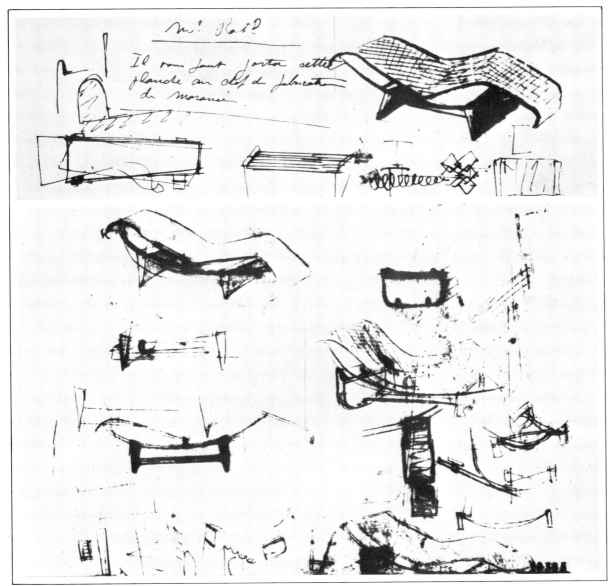

Chaise-longue à réglage continu:
1, 2, 3.   *Studio sketches*
4.   *Variant for the Immeubles-Villas,* 1922
5.   *Variant for the Villa à Carthage,* 1928
6.   *Variant for the Maison de M. X., Brussels,* 1929

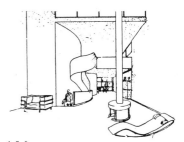

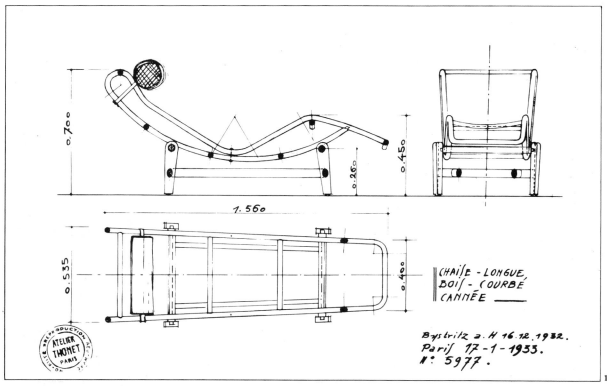

0.700

0.450

0.260

1.560

0.535

0.400

*CHAISE - LONGUE,*
*BOIS - COURBÉ*
*CANNÉE* ———

*Bystritz a. H 16.12.1932.*
*Paris 17-1-1933.*
*N° 5977.*

*Chaise-longue à réglage continu:*
*1. Version in curved wood and bamboo. Experimental model for Thonet, 1932*
*2. Variant in laminated wood for Thonet, 1932*
*3. Version with simplified supporting structure without mesh support, covered in natural-colored canvas, cushion and footrest in natural leather*
*4. Version with structure to support the seat made of metal netting, covered in ponyskin, pedestal lacquered grey-blue and dark grey*

1

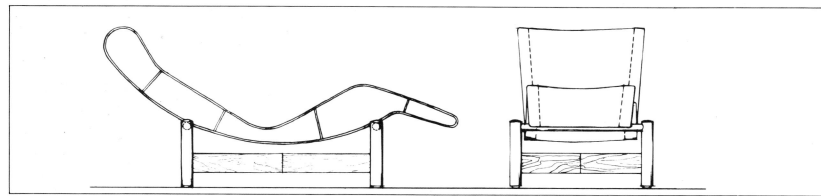

3

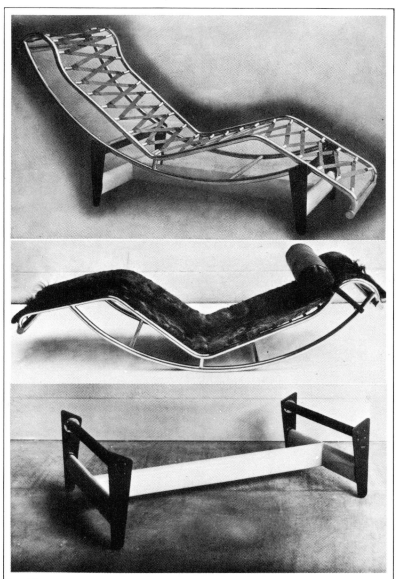

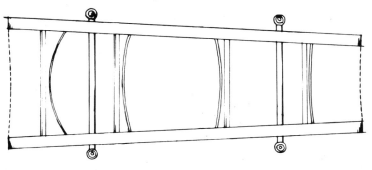

2 4

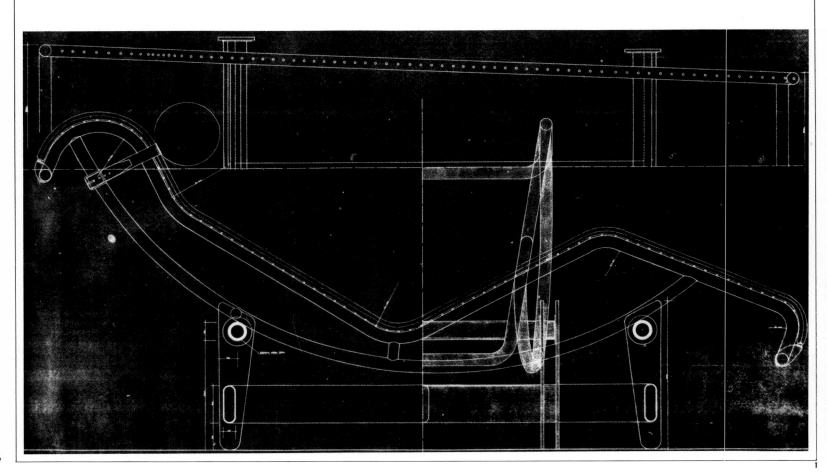

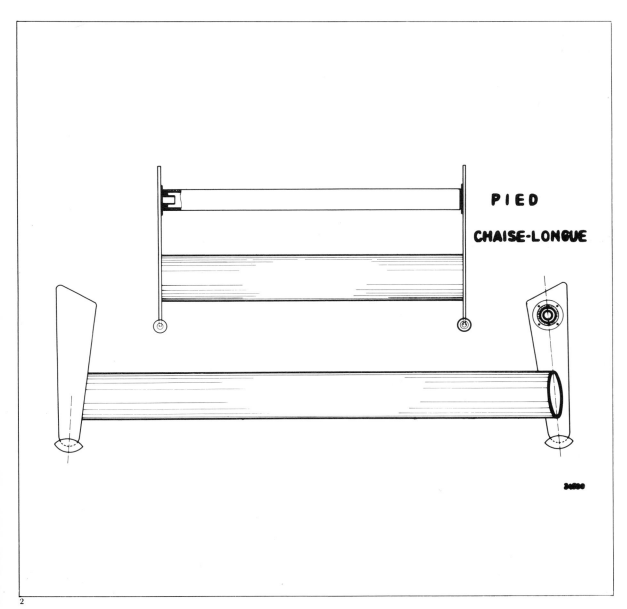

PIED

CHAISE-LONGUE

*Chaise-longue à réglage continu:*
*1. Working drawing for the present-day production*
*2. Working drawing of a plan*          77

2

Le Corbusier, Pierre Jeanneret, Charlotte Perriand

**5 Canapé, 1935**
(73 x 198 x 75 cm)

Production: Cassina, 1974

This model was built for Le Corbusier's home in Rue Nungesser et Coli, Paris.
The chrome-plated steel frame holds together a group of cushions, as in the "Fauteuil grand confort."
In a design taken up by the Fondation Le Corbusier, the divan is planned with several variants: the length is a repeatable unit of 120 cm, the metal support is intended to have horizontal red-lacquered frames and violet vertical frames, and the cushions are in "gros tissage" fabric.
By a linking system at either end it is possible to add more individual pieces to build up a divan of indefinite length.

*1, 2, 3. Version in nickel-plated steel, wool fabric cushions. Cassina, 1974*

78

1

2, 3

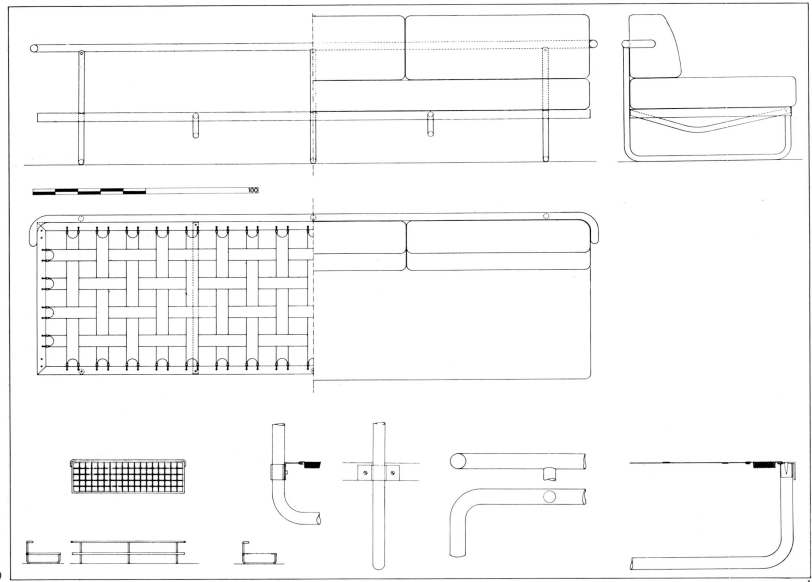

1

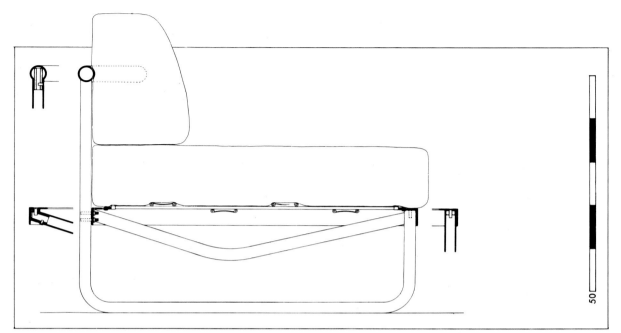

2, 3

*Canapé:*
*1, 2.    Working drawings for present-day production*
*3.    Version with repeatable elements*

50

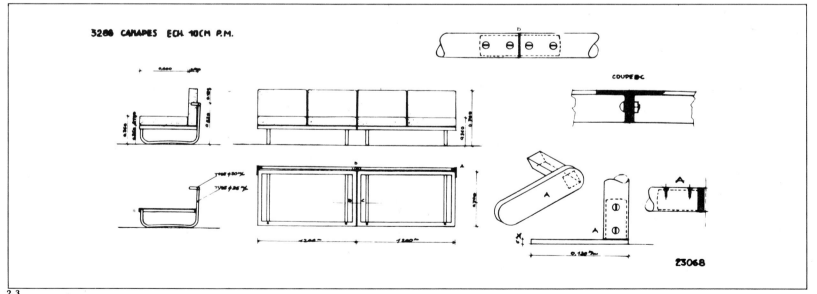

3288 CANAPES ECH 10CM P.M.

COUPE B-C

23068

81

Equipement intérieur d'une habitation, Salon d'Automne, Paris, 1929

Le Corbusier, Pierre Jeanneret, Charlotte Perriand

**6 Table en tube d'avion, section ovoide, 1929**
(69 x 225 x 85 cm)

Production: Cassina, 1974

A glass top colored gold or transparent white rests on a pedestal of black-lacquered or metallic grey steel.
As for the 1928 furniture, the basic idea is the distinction—this time in an inverse relationship—between the supporting and supported elements: in the original plan the four hinges control the height and at the same time create distance between the heavy support and the thin rectangular plane.

*1, 3. Version with black polished steel support and wooden top. Cassina, 1974*
*2. Version with black polished steel support and glass top. Cassina, 1974*

82

1

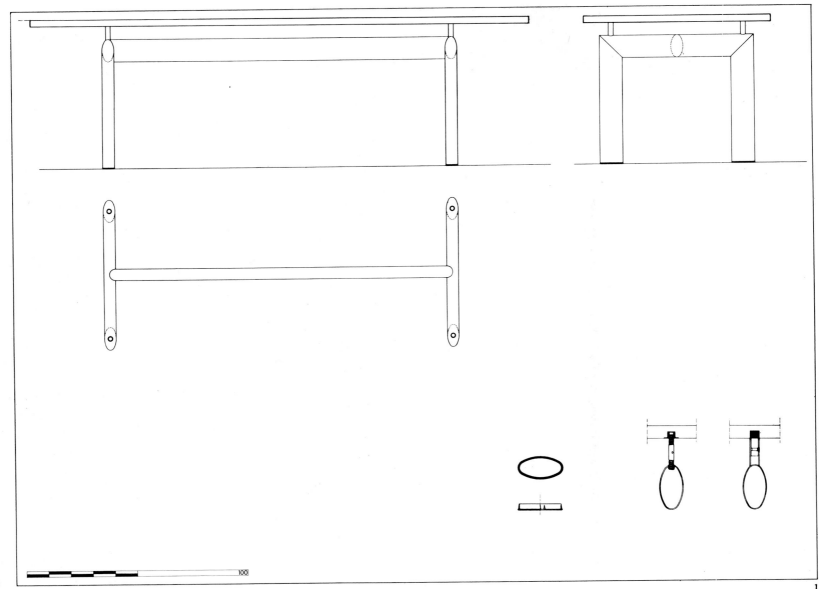

100

*Table en tube d'avion, section ovoïde:*
1. *Working drawings for present-day production*
2, 3. *Present versions with glass or wooden tops, Cassina, 1974*
4. *Model exhibited in the Salon d'Automne of 1929, with metallic grey lacquered pedestal and gold-colored glass top*

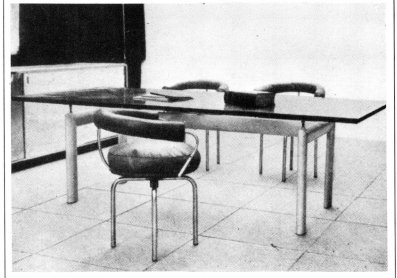

2

3, 4

Le Corbusier, Pierre Jeanneret, Charlotte Perriand

**7 Table dalle de marbre posée sur piètement acier et fonte laquée, 1934**
(70 x 215 x 80 cm)

A block of granite or cipolin marble 4.5 cm thick rests on two "stilts" of lacquered iron. Here too one may speak of two components of one sign, the "supporting" and the "supported."

*1, 2.   Prototype and working drawings*

1

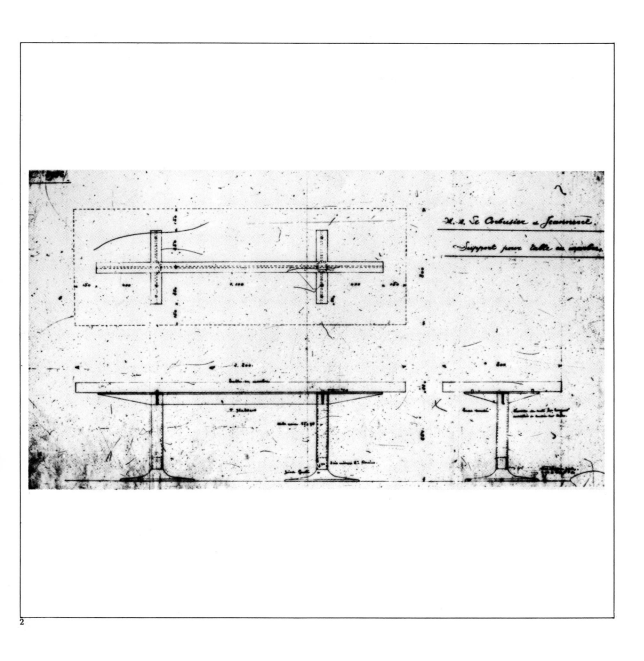

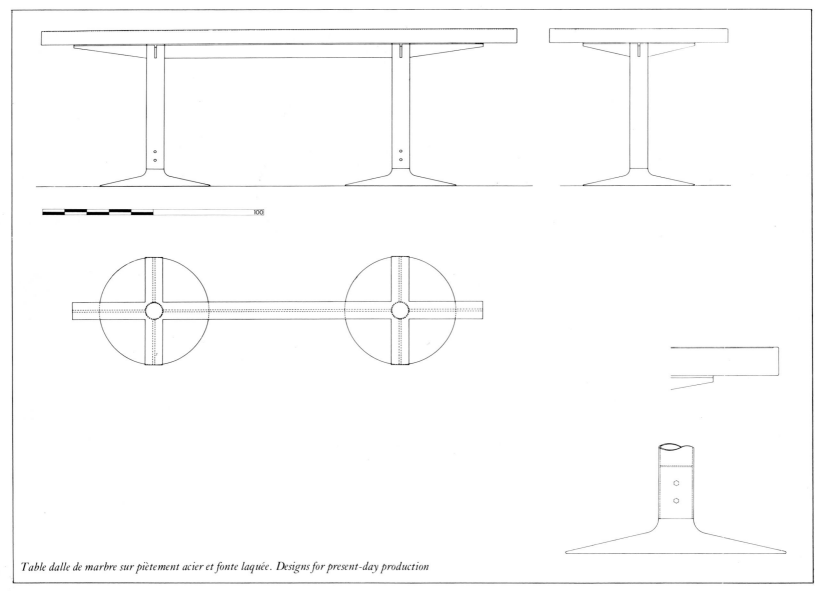

*Table dalle de marbre sur piètement acier et fonte laquée. Designs for present-day production*

*Table dalle de marbre sur piètement acier et fonte laquée. Details of pedestal and top*

Equipement intérieur d'une habitation, Salon d'Automne, Paris, 1929

Le Corbusier, Pierre Jeanneret,
Charlotte Perriand

**8 Siège tournant (Fauteuil), 1929**
(64 x 52 x 52 cm)

**9 Siège tournant (Tabouret), 1929**
(43 x 33 cm)

Between the "signified" element of
the horizontal and the vertical "signifying" element there is a curve which
in its turn leads into the swivel
mechanism.
The back of the "Siège tournant" is a
tube covered in padded leather,
traversed right at the center by a
metal tube attaching it to the seat, and
illustrates another feature of Le Corbusier's design, where the obviousness of the solution recalls an *objet-
trouvé* or a certain *Je-m'en-foutisme*,
somewhat resembling Dadaism.

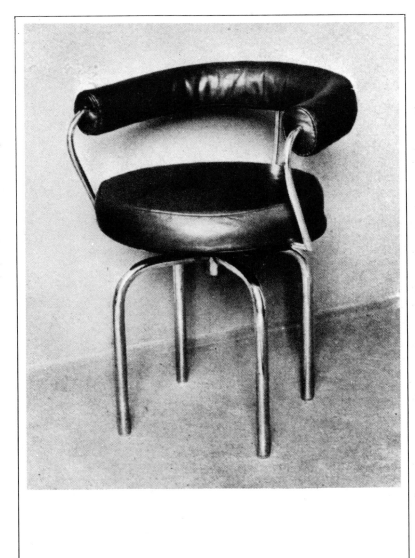

90

*Equipement intérieur d'une habitation, Salon d'Automne, 1929. Living room*

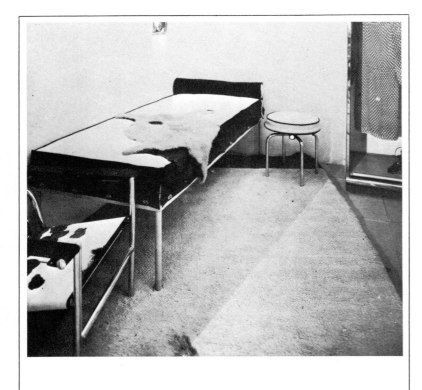

*Bedroom stool, Salon d'Automne, 1929*

1, 2. *Bathroom stool with removable seat. Model prepared for L'Equipement intérieur d'une habitation at the 1929 Salon d'Automne*
3. *Poster advertising Thonet, reproduced here in life-size, for the bathroom stool*

1

2

N° B. 305

Modèle Le Corbusier, P. Jeanneret, Ch. Perriand

3

*Table with metal support and top of natural wood, 1959 (?)*

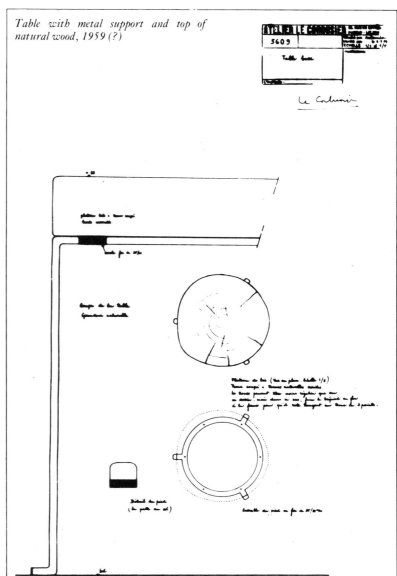

Equipement intérieur d'une habitation, Salon d'Automne, Paris, 1929

Le Corbusier, Pierre Jeanneret, Charlotte Perriand

**10 Meubles acier (Casiers modulés), 1928**
(measurements of the "Modulor")

The standard units made their first appearance in the Esprit Nouveau pavilion in Paris in 1925: they represented an immature experiment in dividing one living area from another by means of standard parallelepipeds supported by plain metal tubing legs.
Standard cupboard units which can be assembled to fit into a wall, stand against it or divide one living area from another. They create the maximum usable space inside them, leaving the maximum space to the room. Beds, tables and chairs, especially, remain masters of the field, which is completely bare of other forms of containers, and function as sculptures in space.

*1. Schéma dei Casiers-types, axonometric drawing for the assembly of the metal sections*
*2. Casiers modulés for the kitchen, Salon d'Automne, 1929*
*3. Casiers modulés, living room wall, Salon d'Automne, 1929*
*4. Study for the "Equipement intérieur d'une habitation" pavilion, Salon d'Automne, 1929*

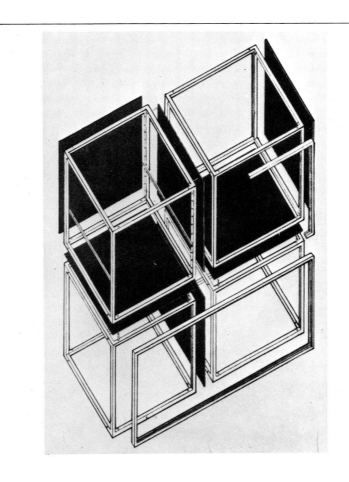

1

*Plan of standard units.*
*The framework is made of racks to take the grooves for drawers, writing slides or mirrors, and permits of a free arrangement of horizontal divisions.*
*Closing apparatus is grooved with sliding doors for two or three units.*
*Metal sheets for partitioning.*

*Various aspects of standard unit elements:*
*1. Units used to partition the bedroom from the lounge (bedroom side)*
*2. Units on which cooking utensils are hung (a horizontal division is provided for the rational arrangement of saucepans) and units for the storage of food*
*3. Units used to partition the kitchen from the dining room (dining room side)*

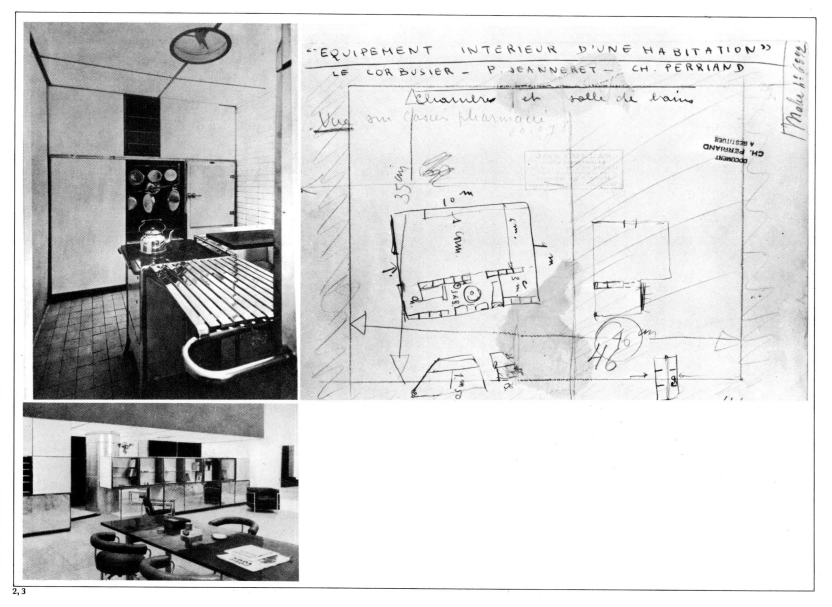

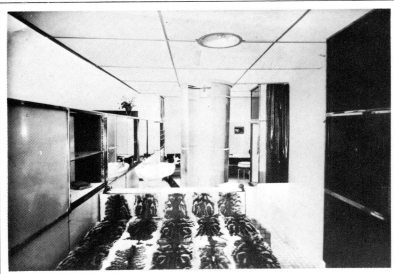

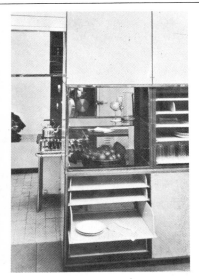

*1, 2. Salon d'Automne, 1929. Casiers
modulés for bedroom and bathroom
3. Salon d'Automne, 1929. Casiers
modulés, detail of the entrance to the
kitchen
4. Salon d'Automne, 1929. Casiers
modulés, detail of the living room*

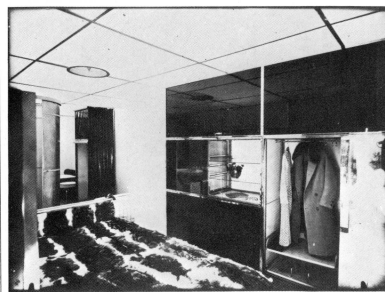

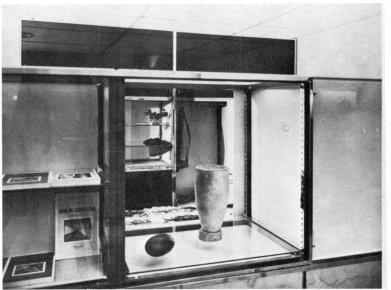

1, 2

3, 4

Eléments mobiliers d'un appartement de jeune homme, International Exhibition, Brussels, 1935. Study.

Le Corbusier, Pierre Jeanneret, Charlotte Perriand

**11 Casiers modulés (Meubles acier), 1935**
(The use of standard measurements arose out of research for the Esprit Nouveau pavilion, 1925, and the Salon d'Automne, 1929.)

An innovation of high precision and infinite technical resources, with possibilities for three-dimensional and sentimental expression
By their nature they are a hybrid: neither an "architectonic sign" nor iconic signs.
They belong to the sphere of architecture as much as to design.
Their stereometric body is comparable to the "Cartesian" part of the buildings, while the anomalous and "brutalist" supports, like so many examples of stilts, belong to the free forms of three-dimensional purist origin.

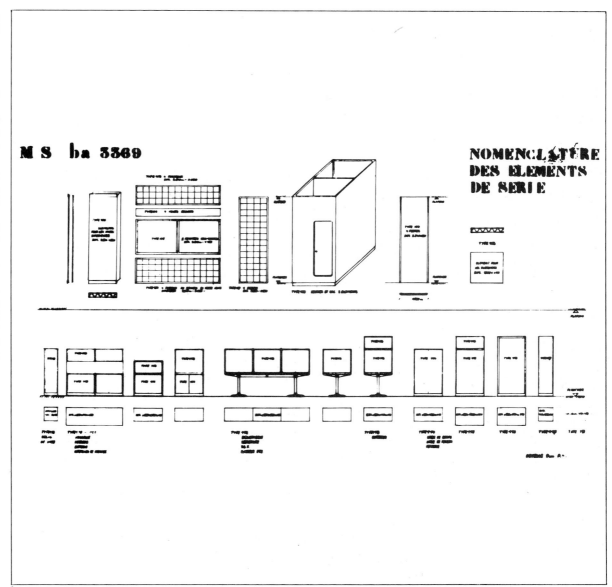

*1. Unit series, working drawings*

*Eléments mobiliers d'un appartement de jeune homme, Brussels International Exhibition, 1935:*
*1.   Salle d'étude. Writing table with slate top on stilts. Fauteuil basculant, wood and straw version prepared by Charlotte Perriand*
*2.   Side of a standard feature with zincographic decoration*
*3.   Mass-produced furniture with suggested partitions*

# Le Corbusier and Us

*Article published in L'architetto, No. 10, 1965, on the occasion of Le Corbusier's death*

In a publication addressed mainly to architects it may be assumed that there is no need to give an account of the works and criticism of Le Corbusier, especially as these topics have been explored at length recently in all the daily papers. To speak of him here is justified in my view by the attempt to establish a relationship with his works which each one of us, individually and collectively, has had or will have; I say this not as the result of a reasoned analysis, but—and I hope in this I am interpreting the thought of many people—as a spontaneous reaction to the news of his death.

The generation born around 1930, to which I belong and to which I shall constantly refer, came to know Le Corbusier (with the exception of the *enfants prodiges*) when he enrolled in the Faculty of Architecture. My first awareness of his architecture came from the copy of his *Maison aux Mathes*, and at a time when so many difficulties were associated with the new graphics, we were unsuccessful in fitting into a critical framework, nor were we helped to do so. The fault could not entirely be ascribed to our teachers and helpers, who were so caught up in the events of the prewar and war years that they did not have the opportunity to make a penetrating study of the development of modern architecture. These same professionals were immediately absorbed into the task of reconstruction. They pursued this task with intense activity, and found the ideas of Le Corbusier useful in that they offered prompt and immediate solutions. In Italy, moreover, very little was written about him before 1948: a few book chapters, some magazine articles, and

the small anthology of writings edited by De Carlo. Therefore his ideas were not very well known, or else were misunderstood—his *esprit machiniste* clashed with our idealistic tradition, while his ideal of precision clashed with our generic availability—and because of this he was not known to most Italian architects until very late. Then he took his place as one of the large number of figures and the countless phenomena of the postwar period to be absorbed and assimilated by us as quickly as possible, to make up for lost time. We therefore came to know Le Corbusier at a particular moment in time. All his theories had been formulated long before and his most significant works had already been executed. We appreciated their importance, but placed them within a modern tradition which had ceased to be so relevant, and turned our attention elsewhere. For those of us who were more interested in the political aspects of our profession, Le Corbusier did not seem to be particularly aligned, in the same way as, for instance, Picasso, the living example of *engagement* and of the parallel between the cultural and the political *avant-garde*. Compared with him, Le Corbusier seemed to us to have stayed fixed in the heroic stance of the 1920s–1930s, so close in time yet so remote, when the political choice of the rulers, of ours in particular, was seen as a generic kind of reformism, as radical culturally as it was imprecise in relation to the ideologies of the time, many of which persist until today. A consequence of this attitude was his theory of town planning, founded on a few talented "artistic" intuitions, a

generous and personal gesture which in spite of the calls for a technological culture proved rather impracticable at an interdisciplinary level as well as difficult to prove "scientifically."

To those among us who at the time were attracted mainly by the question of style, and discovered the forms and underlying concepts of abstract art, Le Corbusier appeared an anachronism of the post-Cubist period when viewed beside the Russian Constructivists, the Bauhaus, or De Stijl. We could not find a satisfactory explanation for the unlikely presence of disconnected figurative elements in his paintings and the coarse plasticity which was not found only in the paintings but always apparent even in his works of architecture: it was difficult to understand this in someone who was so impassioned of classicism, geometry and a purist order.

When we were in our early twenties, we visited the building site of his Unité d'Habitation at Marseilles, and could see that this architecture was the result of "patient research," continued over some ten years since the preliminary studies for it had been made, in the Maison Citrohan of 1920, the 1922 *Immeubles-Villas*, the 1925 *Esprit Nouveau* pavilion; and we could see that all of these works formed part of a precise urban design, yet once again Le Corbusier did not coincide with our immediate interests. During those years in Italy, the architects of the generation before our own, and some of the best among them, fought the battle for organic architecture, which among other things meant the updating and rediscovery of the modern Anglo-American tradition. Having to return hurriedly to the origins of this culture, we came across the idea of the garden city—an idea which was the complete antithesis of Le Corbusier's—and the first Italian popular building program took its inspiration from it as explicitly as it could. Then there were other errors and misunderstandings, for example, the transposition of neo-realism from the cinematographic world to the figurative arts and architecture; much mention was made, often inappropriately, of a popular national language, and this certainly did not bring us any nearer to the radical cosmopolitanism of Le Corbusier.

Finally, our knowledge and acceptance of him in Italy were conditioned by the approaches and dates of publication of the two most important books on the history of modern architecture. It was in 1950 that Zevi published his *Storia dell'Architettura Moderna*, a work preceded by two other essays, all of which were legitimately presented according to the personal viewpoint of the author, who had lived through the American architectural experience and whose historical account superseded *Spazio, tempo e architettura* by Giedion, a member of the CIAM and a historian of rationalism. Unfortunately for us, the latter book, which is certainly preparatory to Zevi's, was not translated into Italian until 1954 although published in 1941.

It was not until the mid-1950s that our generation began to appreciate the work of Le Corbusier fully. This came about as a result of the "Casabella" studies directed by Rogers; following the tradition of the CIAM and published in the Italian cities of greatest European interest, they carefully followed the work of Le Corbusier and recorded its present relevance.

This derived less from the intense working life of Le Corbusier than from the fact that he was seen in a new light within a social and cultural condition which embraced all of us. Of course, it was not given to everyone to have the wonderful and exceptional opportunity of building the capital of the Punjab; but since the new society in which many of us had believed had come to naught and the more complex road of parliamentary democracy been chosen, we all found ourselves working in a dialectical condition which was the more harsh the greater was the radicalism of the world of architecture and the wider was the gap between lofty ideas and the defense of those institutions which abandoned their traditional position only where they succeeded in making a larger profit.

When we considered his personal language, we found in the 1950s that the continuity—it must be repeated—of the style of Le Corbusier encompassed and solved many problems which were common to the whole world of the figurative arts. The (temporary) conflict between abstract and figurative art, the birth of informal art, a rethinking of Expressionism, even the brutalism of the so-called art of *reportage* and of what today is defined as a new figuration—all these phenomena were anticipated in Chandigarh, in the Convent of La Tourette, and above all in the Ronchamp Chapel. For each of these schools of art it is possible to find in the most recent work of Le Corbusier a precedent, an exemplification, a model. And, as has been said, it may be that the only attribute of any value which can be established in contemporary art criticism is the paradigmatic value of the work produced, in other words, the work of art serving as a model for other works which, even if they are not artistic, are at least expressive of a culture.

However, the paradigmatic nature of Le Corbusier's example does not relate to his architecture alone, although his buildings have inspired excellent followers in all parts of the world, but to his activity as a whole, to the totality of his theory and practice which are indissolubly fused as they have never been in the case of anyone else. So that while the creative activity of the old architect amazed us all, it is true too that his theories have been shown to be well founded, and in our own time we have seen his forecasts come true, obviously with a degree of approximation, in the so-called consumer society, which shows uncertainty or indifference towards certain ideological values while being very clear as to its primary and quantitative demands. But apart from these considerations (which would necessitate an examination of those ideas which were formulated in order to solve social problems and which later became the reality of an undifferentiated mass culture: that is, we would have to ask ourselves how far creative artists are to be held responsible for the degeneration of their ideas and language—a question which would be a digression here), the old ideas held by Le Corbusier have stood up to the passage of time and to the conditions of various countries better than others. His insistence on the irreplaceable social and cultural value of the city, his design for grand concepts, the conflict between Utopia and reality as an aim for which to proceed, these are the terms of our dilemma today.

But a distinction must be made here. In spite of coincidences in theme, the way of thought and especially the way of putting his architecture into effect, the design of Le Corbusier and the town planning are perhaps the opposite of our discussing and carrying out these same things in a bureaucratic and "realistic" manner. While the German or Dutch rationalists may have worked together with local council officials when they drew up their plans and then put them into effect with technical efficiency, Le Corbusier's position does not stand up to the scrutiny of the economic commissions, and it is incompatible with bureaucratic administration (not to be understood from a "man-in-the-street" point of view) until the day arrives when it becomes capable of using unorthodox creative energy without crushing it.

The professional difficulties suffered by Le Corbusier do not derive from the obvious contradictions between art and practice, but from the special peculiarities of his message. In short, those points which distinguished him from others, but imitable nevertheless, because in my opinion they best exemplify his contribution, are the universality, objectivity and simplicity of his points of reference; many of them can be quoted. In *Vers une architecture* he wrote in defense of the standard unit: "All men have a similar organism and similar functions. All men have similar needs." In *The Map of Athens* he stated that the four functions of town planning must be based on that same number of universal needs: a home, work, transport and education. He provided an even more inadequate reason to oppose the concept of residential decentralization and the necessity for commuting which this entails: "The solar cycle is short, its twenty-four hours fatally govern the activities of man, establishing the limits of his movements."

Of course, all this can be reexamined from a more complex viewpoint than his own. But among all the ambiguity, which he elevated to a system, it must be recognized that few figures have remained so constant in their positions as Le Corbusier (with all the limitations this comprises). This explains why he is now being rediscovered, at a time when our own excessively mobile architectural culture is turning from the tortuous and often whimsical paths it has followed and has decided that there is a case for re-evaluating Utopian models.

Having reduced and exemplified the problems in their extreme terms, Le Corbusier found the methods best suited to making them generally acceptable; he understood the enormous persuasive power of slogans and saw the importance of presenting them in visual form before the man in the street and the administrators. "What is needed at all costs is a line of conduct neither excessively nor insufficiently developed in detail because it is necessary and must be sufficient."

In spite of this, his method, just because of its far-seeing objectivity, was always in conflict with the economic and administrative powers. On the other hand, how could it have been possible for his radical view to coexist with the obstructive factors, whose role in every type of society is to complicate matters, impose restrictions and invent irrational procedures? Why should anyone find this surprising?

From the point of view of his architecture, among those of us who are professors in this field Le Corbusier's concentration on the essential has with few exceptions encountered some opposition because of our liking for complexity, for the construction of artificial and harmful factions, an irrational personal attitude, and the vast gap between our theory and practice. In other words, if Le Corbusier fought against all that is academic and bureaucratic, against the harmful profit motive and against stupidity carried to the lengths of brutality, most of us on the other hand have either become part of the economic and bureaucratic machine or else oppose it in the name of an incomprehensible intellectualism which in the long run results only in isolating us.

Naturally, in this conflict between creative vitality and the groups that wield power (and there is no need to repeat that this applies equally to the social sphere) Le Corbusier was bound to emerge the loser from a practical standpoint, as is confirmed by his recent statements which are far from optimistic. And here too we find the key to a choice of direction and behavior. As is often the case, the story of Le Corbusier reminds us of two possibilities to bet on, the immediate one and the long-term one, for "there is no such thing as a large or small invention, only large or small consequences."

*Renato de Fusco*